Students into Teachers

THE STUDENTS LIBRARY OF EDUCATION

Students into Teachers

Experiences of Probationers in Schools

by Mildred Collins
University of Leicester

LONDON
ROUTLEDGE & KEGAN PAUL
NEW YORK: THE HUMANITIES PRESS

First published 1969
by Routledge & Kegan Paul Ltd
Broadway House, 68–74 Carter Lane
London, E.C.4

Printed in Great Britain
by Northumberland Press Limited
Gateshead

SBN 7100 6338 5 (C)
SBN 7100 6342 3 (P)

Volumes dealing with curriculum studies, methodology
and other more general topics are the responsibility of
the General Editor, Professor Tibble.

THE STUDENTS LIBRARY OF EDUCATION has been designed to meet the needs of students of Education at Colleges of Education and at University Institutes and Departments. It will also be valuable for practising teachers and educationists. The series takes full account of the latest developments in teacher-training and of new methods and approaches in education. Separate volumes will provide authoritative and up-to-date accounts of the topics within the major fields of sociology, philosophy and history of education, educational psychology, and method. Care has been taken that specialist topics are treated lucidly and usefully for the non-specialist reader. Altogether, the Students' Library of Education will provide a comprehensive introduction and guide to anyone concerned with the study of education and with educational theory and practice.

As the course in a college or department of Education nears its end, most students will be aware of mixed feelings about the year that faces them, in their first teaching post. On the one hand, they will welcome in anticipation the greater measure of independence and responsibility, both in their work and in their out of school lives; at the same time they will be aware that no course, however good, can have prepared them fully for all the problems and difficulties that they may meet as inexperienced teachers. Will the school they join and the children they are to be responsible for be like those they have experienced in their school practices? How will they be received by their colleagues on the staff? What kind of person will the Head be and how much help can they expect as novices in their first post? How will their success be judged and by whom? They will know from experience or hearsay or reading that there are difficult schools and difficult children—difficult even for experienced teachers. Some of their trepidations may well turn out to have been unjustified but they will not for some time be in a position to distinguish between fantasy and reality in this matter.

We should all agree about two things. First that the college course should include in its preparation of the student a realistic picture of the situation, both objective and subjective, that the beginner has to cope with. Secondly that support and guidance should be available over the period of the probationary year and indeed beyond it where it is needed.

For both these services Dr. Mildred Collins' book should be of value, both to students and young teachers themselves and to those who can help them. What she has to say is based on surveys of conditions of work and the reactions of young teachers to them. She deals with the network of relationships in the society of the school and with the images and stereotypes which influence these relationships. Reference is made throughout to the evidence on which the findings are based and the frequency of occurrence of conditions, attitudes and assumptions is clearly stated. Certainly the student who reads this book will have a more realistic picture of the task that lies ahead and to that extent be better prepared for it.

J.W.T.

Contents

CONTENTS

Acknowledgements

I should like to thank all those who answered my questionnaires: Chief Education Officers, Principals of Colleges, Professors of Education, Heads of Schools, and, especially, the probationers in schools. I am most grateful for all the help which I received. I hope that I have not misused any of the information kindly given. Inevitably my attitude will not always be the same as that of the person quoted.

I should also like to take this opportunity of thanking Professor Tibble for encouraging me to write this book.

M.C.

Introduction

This book is intended for students and probationers in schools, and for those people who try to help them. It aims to capture the first-hand experiences of probationers set against a background of general information about probation, and comments from heads of schools and chief education officers. Finally, certain suggestions are put forward for making probation more satisfying, both for new teachers and the profession as a whole. However, readers of the book, having considered the evidence, may come to different conclusions. In the meantime, it is hoped that the picture presented will comfort some probationers by showing them that their experiences are not unique; it will alert others to possible difficulties; and suggest why those who are happy and successful might be expected to be so. It should also provide an opportunity for probationers to see how academic knowledge helps in the understanding of school situations.

Heads of schools and teachers, local education authority officials and tutors of colleges and departments can compare their views and information about probationers, and relate their own efforts to help them with what other people say they do.

Most of the information presented in this book has been obtained from three researches, some details of which are given below.

The *Aberdeen* University Department of Education and College of Education enquiry, which was carried out in 1962, and reported, in a privately published booklet, *The First Two Years of Teaching*, in 1963, by R. P. Clark and J. D. Nisbet. The organisation of the Scottish educational system and the qualifications required for teachers differ from ours, but it is possible to recognise fairly easily the English equivalents.

In this research, 76 men and 166 women returned completed questionnaires (a 73% response from the 1960 year group of the Aberdeen College of Education). Just less than 50% were graduates, and 37% of the total of 242 had done their two-year probationary period in primary schools.

The *Birmingham* University Institute of Education College Research Group also conducted their enquiry in 1962. This was among 2,000 teachers who had left nine colleges in the Birmingham A.T.O. in 1960-61 and 1961-62. A privately published report, *The Probationary Year*, by J. Cornwell, appeared in 1965.

This was based on replies to questionnaires received from 1,169 probationers, of whom 104 men and 500 women were working in primary schools, and 233 men and 332 women were in secondary schools.

The Heads of schools employing 500 of these probationers were asked to complete exactly the same questionnaire as the probationers: 108 replied.

A *Leicester* University School of Education enquiry to graduates who had left this university in 1960, 1961 and 1962 to take up teaching, and to the Heads of the schools in which they had taught. This research took place from 1961 to 1963 and then was extended in 1964 and 1965 to include L.E.A. officers and heads of colleges, departments and institutes of education concerned with helping probationers. Only a small part of this enquiry has been reported before, by M. Collins (1964), so that much of the information in this book is new.

In the original enquiry to probationers, replies were received from 221 men and 176 women, of whom 93 were untrained graduates. This represented a 70% response from the untrained teachers and 73% response from the trained. Of those who responded 215 had spent their first year in grammar schools, 68 in modern, 34 in comprehensive and 30 in primary schools; the remainder had gone into colleges of further education, small private schools, etc., and were excluded from the analysis of the results.

The Heads of the probationers' schools were sent a short questionnaire asking about the probationers' progress during the first year; 304 replied, 208 from grammar, 49 from modern, 31 from comprehensive and 16 from primary schools. When the enquiry was extended in 1964 and 1965 by sending out additional questionnaires of a different kind, 117 Chief Education Officers or Directors of Education responded (73% of the total number), and so did members of 18 university institutes and 28 departments and colleges of education.

All the questionnaires sent out from Leicester included open-ended questions. The answers to these provided a rich harvest of comment on the probationary year.

A glance at the numbers of probationers, their qualifications, and the schools involved in these three researches shows that each provides for the others something of a check, and at the same time, extends the field of enquiry. For example, the Birmingham research relates to college trained probationers only; the Leicester solely to graduates, but the Aberdeen includes both. From Leicester, less than 10% of the probationers taught in primary schools; from Aberdeen less than 40%, while from Birmingham, it was over half.

References in this book to these researches and to the

persons included in them are by the name of origin only; that is, 'Aberdeen', 'Birmingham' and 'Leicester'. An Aberdeen probationer, for example, means one who trained there and was included in the enquiry: he may, or may not, have been teaching in Aberdeen. 'He' may also have been female. The conventional masculine form is used in order to make the account run more smoothly. For a similar reason, very occasionally, the source of a quotation is not given in the text, but in all these cases, it can be assumed that the quotation has been taken from the Leicester research.

From time to time, of course, researches outside these three are used to supply evidence, and references are also made to recordings of discussion groups with probationers. Altogether, something is known of the teaching experiences of about 2,000 probationers. It remains to be seen how far these confirm our expectations or surprise us by their unexpectedness. They provide a basis for discussion on the purpose of the probationary year.

1

The 'period of initiation'

Changing ideas on the probationary year

'Alone at last!'—well, not really—alone with thirty-five younger children or thirty older ones, not to mention other members of staff. This exclamation nevertheless expresses the feelings of many newly qualified teachers as they start out on their first job, tasting the 'pleasures of financial independence, the joy of being one's own boss'—to quote from comments of the Leicester probationers who replied to questionnaires on their first year experiences. Perhaps this is one of the reasons why the thought of a visit from an H.M.I. or an L.E.A. adviser, or even the Head of the school arouses such mixed feelings during the probationary year. In spite of having completed his training and having the status of a qualified teacher, the probationer feels himself to be on trial: the probationary year still has to be passed.

Nevertheless, not all first year teachers are visited, or inspected; for example over 50% of the 397 Leicester probationers, who began teaching in 1961 and 1962, were left alone both by H.M.I.'s and local advisers and inspectors. Whether or not the probationer was visited depended very much on the type of school in which he had chosen to teach. However, not only did some probationers receive no visits from inspectors or advisers, they received no visits from Heads or fellow teachers either. There may be good reasons for this, as we shall see later. As one new teacher put it: 'My preparation books in my probationary year were never inspected and my lessons were never attended by any other member of staff, including the Headmaster—who was supposed to be guiding me. Whilst this gave me great relief, I do not consider it a very satisfactory state of affairs.' This comment is interesting for, while revealing an undesirable situation, it also points to the recognition that visits by Heads and inspectors have important purposes, in addition to finding out how well or badly, the new teacher is getting on. Fifty years ago, any visit to a probationer's class would have been seen only in terms of passing or failing—terms in which many people still see the probationary year.

This view is no longer acceptable. The probationary year is, or should be, much more than this. In the pamphlet *Teachers in their First Posts* (1961, p. 2) issued by the N.U.T. and A.T.C.D.E., probation is defined as a bridge period, 'both the beginning of true professional responsibilities and the last phase of initial training'. This stress on the first year's teaching as a continuation of college and university training is new, and most important from the point of view of helping the new teacher to be as good as possible, and for the status of teaching as a profession.

Probation and the professional status of teaching

The ideas of probation and professional status may at first seem incompatible, yet we are quite used to the idea of probationer, or some alternative name, in connection with many professions. The would-be solicitor serves a period in a solicitor's office, the university assistant lecturer's appointment comes up for the sessional review, and we all know the medical student who walks the hospital wards, and the probationary nurse. We may not know that the

H.M.I. who visits us has a two-year probationary period too. In all these cases, with the exception of the university lecturer, the probationers are taught a great deal of their professional expertise during the probationary period. The stress is on probation as a time of learning and the various professions take responsibility for the training of their new recruits.

Some professions also keep a register of their members. The General Medical Council is perhaps the most generally known of these professional associations, because the enforcement of its ethical standard is often brought sharply, if briefly, to the notice of the public, by the report of someone being 'struck off' the register. This suggests a concept of professionalism, extending beyond sheer physical and intellectual competence, and including certain social and ethical attitudes. There are certain expectations about the general behaviour of teachers also, though the teaching profession has no register of members. Nevertheless, it is important that teachers should accept more responsibility for the training and admission of new members of the profession.

Probation and the Department of Education and Science

When in the second half of the last century, the State took on the burden of financing the greater part of the educational system, the Department of Education laid down a system for approving the teachers who worked in schools. This procedure has changed much over the years and now differs according to whether the teacher has taken a recognised course of professional training or whether the teacher possesses other qualifications, such as a university degree, which make him eligible for qualified teacher status. For the professionally trained teacher the decision as to his acceptability is left to the employing authority

3

which informs the Secretary of State; this method is called procedure A. Procedure B is the method used with un-trained personnel: here the reports for or against accept-ability are from H.M.I's who likewise inform the Secretary of State. In procedure B there is more direct state control through the H.M.I.'s and less local responsibility. If a pro-bationer has not reached an acceptable degree of com-petence, whether under procedure A or B, then his probation will be extended for a further six months: very rarely is he asked to leave the profession immediately at the end of his probationary year. He is given a second, third, or even a fourth, chance. The recommendations for extension of probation under procedure B are three times as great under procedure A: in 1961-2 they were 9.3% compared with 3.6% for probationers under procedure A. This is not unexpected for probationers assessed under procedure B are untrained. Any new teacher whether trained or untrained who feels that he has been unfairly judged can challenge the evidence against him, preferably through his professional association.

The responsibilities of the L.E.A. and the schools

This transfer of responsibility for the approval of new teachers from the central to the local authority and school began some time ago. In the 1940s, H.M.I.'s used to visit and approve—or not approve (to the extent of 7% in 1947) —the practical proficiency of the teachers, and teachers approved were given a certificate of recognition. The part played by local authorities was minimal. In 1949 there was a change: the local education authority was charged with the responsibility of assessing the effectiveness of the teacher and when this was not up to standard, of making a special report to the Minister. Ten years later, in 1959, in Administrative Memorandum 4/59 from the Ministry

4

of Education to the local authorities, the Minister reiterated the point about the responsibility for the probationary year being with the employing authority. In addition the memorandum contained suggestions about guidance and placement in schools and about helping students in difficulties. But it gave no indication that the year was to be thought of as a continuation of training. Indeed, it was still thought of largely in terms of shipwreck and rescue. The new conception of probation as a continuation of training has been put forward by the teachers and the colleges and departments of education.

This is a radical change and will require a similar change in attitude on the part of many people, local advisers and inspectors, H.M.I.'s, Heads of schools, college and department tutors and last, but not least, teachers themselves. Old habits die hard. A probationer reported: 'I received an inspector's visit only as a formality. My impression was that one should keep one's fingers crossed not to be caught out during probation.'

In fact, a local inspector's rôle is only marginally concerned with inspection, with passing or failing teachers. He is primarily concerned with helping schools to develop. His main function is to 'interpret to teachers and to the public the educational policy of the authorities, and modern educational ideas and methods, and also to interpret to the competent authorities the experiences, needs and aspirations of teachers and local communities' (Edmonds, 1961, p. 86). He can be viewed as an educational go-between. The L.E.A.'s and their officers obviously have a crucial rôle to play in the refashioning of the probationary year.

The rôle of colleges and departments of education

The statement just quoted on the function of inspectors, with its reference to 'modern educational ideas and

5

methods', indicates an overlapping field with colleges and departments. The N.U.T. states in *Teachers in their First Posts* (N.U.T. and A.T.C.D.E. 1961, p. 2) that 'it is the duty of the colleges and departments to be at all times in the fore-front of educational thought, constantly engaged in experiment.' It is obviously important that there should be close liaison between the inspectorate and the colleges and departments of education. At the moment this liaison appears somewhat cool. Some inspectors make contact with the college if a former student gets into difficulties, but this is by no means common; in some people's minds it raises the question of professional confidentiality. How far by going outside the school should one make a new teacher's weaknesses professionally public? How far should the care and responsibility of the department of college be extended?

Some people feel that it is ethically wrong to make enquiries about former students; to quote from one college principal who replied to the Leicester enquiry: 'I felt it a very delicate matter to follow old students of college who had now the status of "teacher" into their schools.' This is an acknowledgement of a very important change, 'the step forward in life', which colleges are right to take seriously and not wish to blur. But it also suggests an over-sensitivity to the status of the new teacher. It seems right that the integration of the former student with his profession should be left to the school and its advisers and inspectors, yet that this should entail a complete lack of communication between colleges and departments of former students seems wholly undesirable. At the very least it would be useful to know whether ideas about training are effective in practice.

Probationers working for different L.E.A.'s

In 1965 an enquiry was made among Directors of Educa-

6

tion and Chief Education Officers in England and Wales about conditions for probationers in their area: 117, or 71% replied to this Leicester enquiry. It was interesting to see something of the varying situations in different localities. The proportion of probationers among the teaching staff turned out to be very uneven. One rural L.E.A. had none: 'We try not to get involved in the employment of probationers in view of our isolation and small schools with few facilities.' This was an exception, however, for most rural areas were involved and up to 3% of their school staff were probationers. This contrasts with nine authorities in heavily industrialised zones in which probationers made up approximately 10% of the full-time teaching staff. More commonly the proportion in industrial areas was 7%. One third of the probationers who began teaching in September 1964 obtained posts in these localities.

The amount of help given to probationers by the L.E.A.'s also varied from area to area. The majority of L.E.A.'s sent advisers or local inspectors to assist the schools with new teachers, but about a quarter left this almost entirely to individual schools. A typical reply from such an area was: 'The Head is responsible for probationers with any additional assistance, where required, from the Assistant Director and Physical Education organiser. In cases of exceptional difficulty, the advice of H.M. Inspectors would be sought.' It is doubtful whether this and similar arrangements represent a positive policy towards school responsibility. It seems more likely that these unsatisfactory arrangements are forced on authorities through lack of suitable advisers or because the schools are widely scattered. This is especially to be regretted in the case of rural schools for several Education Officers mentioned the problem of the teaching Head in a small country school with no free time to give to the probationer, and the

7

isolation of the probationer himself, both within the school community 'an absence of kindred spirits' (to quote one Education Officer), and within the surrounding local community with 'its impoverished cultural life'. Visits from advisers and organisers would seem essential in these cases. Indeed, in some rural communities the visits are frequent. In one, for example, there were routine visits each term and at monthly intervals when required.

Many authorities recognise that there are limits to the help which their visiting inspectors and advisers can give. As one said:

> Under present staffing restrictions, probationers have to go immediately into fully responsible posts and these are often in small schools where the Headmaster is involved in teaching. In practice able probationers overcome this and gain from the highly personal relationships of such a school. Weaker ones find it difficult and we are aware that they are not receiving necessary help.

One Education Officer (without school advisers) drew attention to another difficulty: 'If all teachers on probation were teaching in infant schools they could be dealt with by one method. It happens, however, that our particular major collection of probationer teachers are at one single grammar school this year; in any case there is little in common between the requirements of a teacher on probation who never goes outside the laboratory at one of the grammar schools and the teacher on probation who never sees anything outside a reception class.' Practically all other L.E.A.'s in their replies ignored this problem of probationers with different needs, possibly because they tend to solve it by not considering themselves particularly responsible for the probationers in grammar schools.

New teachers in direct grant and independent grammar schools or in colleges of further education do not have a

8

probationary period, whereas in maintained grammar schools new teachers are as much on probation as are beginners in other maintained schools. Nevertheless, they have fewer visits from local advisers and inspectors, probably because originally these schools were inspected chiefly, if not solely, by H.M.I.'s. The Head of the grammar school may not appear to have much responsibility for the probationer either, who may, indeed, be unaware that he is on probation. In fact the Head, as in other schools, has to submit a report on his progress, the form and number of these reports varying from one authority to another.

Guidance within the schools

The help which Leicester probationers received from their colleagues inside the school was variable and their comments provide a picture of widely differing situations. Many probationers could echo the new teacher in a secondary modern school who said: 'The whole staff (about 24) were very ready to offer help or advice if, and when, it was needed on any point at all (ready in a friendly way, not critical)', or the one who described his guidance as 'more worldly wisdom than help'. Some probationers worked with colleagues in positions of mutual respect, where 'Consultation on all matters has been very free and friendly', 'burdens shared equally', and 'I voluntarily showed my exam papers to the Senior mistress, but I need not have done so'. This attitude of equality 'I need not have done so' can and in some cases did, slip over into a condition where too little was asked for, offered, or received: 'I have had informal discussions with people on the staff with whom I am friendly. Generally speaking though, my first year was very much a sink-or-swim affair.'

On the other hand, some probationers do not want help. They feel that they are getting on well, their training has been completed and they subscribe to the view 'that teaching is an ability which cannot be taught—a person can either teach or he can't and is best left to find his own solution to his problems'. So said one Leicester graduate, very recently a probationer, but wishing to think of himself in other terms. In this he is expressing, more openly than most, a common desire to be a full member of his profession, completely proficient. His colleagues often encourage him in this: 'a probationary teacher wants to be accepted as a full member of staff. Other teachers do this [sic] and in doing so they forget to advise unless specifically asked.'

Some teachers think that advice is useless anyway, an attitude more prevalent amongst men. They believe that there are certain experiences, difficulties, growing pains which must be gone through. This attitude can be unhelpful. This was realised by one young man working in a boys' school who said: 'More help could have been gained if older staff were more willing to accept something could be done rather than as professional hazards [sic].' While there is a kernel of truth in this idea, the necessity of working through problems alone, and of the inability of people to help, there is also an unexpressed feeling that a new teacher should earn his professional status, that difficulties and tribulations are essential and unavoidable parts of the initiation process. The older teacher often remembers his own disappointments and is, secretly and against his better nature, not sorry to see someone else going through the same problems. And some probationers are difficult to help.

On the other hand some probationers expect too much help: 'The Headmaster might have come in to show me group work', and some Heads, particularly primary Heads.

in their anxiety to be sure their teachers are doing well, seem unconsciously to encourage this dependency, they like to be the all-provider: 'Syllabus prepared for all staff by Head'; 'Setting of papers and marking done entirely by Head'; 'Person in charge of ratings'. No doubt this attitude follows from the very few posts of special responsibility in primary schools and the full teaching programmes of the staff, but it sometimes looks as if the pupils in the school include not only the children but the staff too. The staff are not given sufficient professional responsibility. This is not of course confined to primary schools, although most prevalent there. A lack of acceptance of staff competence and responsibility is shown in this comment from a probationer in a grammar school: 'There were no staff meetings, and, in fact, any meetings of teachers were considered almost illegal. The impression given was that the ordinary teacher was unfit to discuss anything.'

Sometimes of course the fault can lie in the teacher's own mistaken impressions. When a probationer makes this remark: 'I found that all new members of staff were not welcome—and it took virtually the whole year to feel part of the common room' one feels at first indignation at such unfriendliness. But on discovering later that this particular probationer found it difficult to make friends outside school too, the picture of the school situation changes. It looks as if the unhappy situation was partly of his own making.

On the whole, Leicester probationers, felt that they were much welcomed and given a good deal of help. There was, however, a thread of disillusionment running through some remarks—almost inevitably so, for what is a very special event for the probationer, 'a real job at last', is for the rest of the staff an annual or terminal occurrence. (It would not be surprising if the welcome sometimes lacked warmth, but it is none the less cooling to the young

teacher for all that). What is clear from the various enquiries is that, in spite of all the power and influence of
Heads in schools, the probationers thought that they got
more help from their fellow teachers than from their
Heads. This is not to say that Heads were parsimonious in
giving help, or that it was not appreciated, but simply that
educationists outside schools (although not the Heads in
them, according to the Birmingham survey) have tended to
under-rate the part played by colleagues, particularly
young colleagues, in helping the new teacher.

The older teacher, whom one would naturally suppose to
be of greater help, does not always turn out to be so. The
probationer has difficulty in identifying with him, as a
person who has had the same problems as himself and
therefore able to offer him useful advice. The probationer
feels much more at home with a new teacher. Relations
between old and new teachers are hampered by the fact
that they may, subconsciously be a threat to each other,
the one through his present skills and the other through
his potentialities for the future. We hear a good deal about
the difficulties of the probationer; for example, in admit-
ting lack of knowledge: 'Don't be afraid to ask advice—
it is not a failure to do so.' Very little is heard about the
difficulties of the older teacher, the necessity of being able
to cope with the feeling that he is about to be surpassed,
that his knowledge and skills are being eroded by new
ideas and the attraction of youthful enthusiasm.

In addition to these psychological difficulties in giving
and accepting help, problems relating to the size and type
of school alter the pattern of help which can be given in
it. This shows clearly in the experiences recorded by the
Leicester probationers who went into practically the whole
range of schools. Those in junior schools received far more
help from the Head than did those in secondary modern
schools, whether in connection with methods of teaching

or with discipline. In grammar schools the Head gave help with discipline but not with teaching methods. In comprehensive schools his rôle had further changed and he was no longer obviously concerned with discipline either, this has been handed over to housemasters, year mistresses, heads of departments, etc. The present trend appears to be for more direct responsibility, more direct power, to pass to non-heads of schools. It is not clear how far L.E.A. advisers, in their desire to help probationers, recognise this.

Some L.E.A. officials—it was apparent from the Leicester research—realise the importance of personal relationships in helping probationers, and believe that Heads 'who have good staff relationships generally are good with probationers'. A few officials seem to put a heavy burden of expectation on what respect for a Head can do for his probationers. On the other hand, many were well aware of how helpful a real concern on the part of the Head can be. One Education officer in the enquiry, but only one, underlined the importance of '*young* Heads'.

Meetings for probationers

In some areas, in addition to visiting schools, L.E.A. officials arrange meetings for probationers although in 1965 71 out of the 117 authorities replying to the Leicester enquiry had no meetings at all. Of these which did, the most common arrangement was to have one meeting at the beginning of the session. This was usually a semi-social affair at which the Education Officer and his assistants took the opportunity of explaining the policy and educational facilities of the area. Such an occasion provided an opportunity for probationers to meet each other. If other meetings were provided they took the form of lectures and discussions.

Institutes of Education sometimes put on courses for

probationary teachers and virtually all have other lectures and discussions which probationers may attend. L.E.A. advisers and inspectors—and Heads of schools—often help with these Institute courses, and one argument in favour of the Institute as a centre for probationers is that it provides neutral meeting ground for these 'interested parties'.

A good deal needs to be done in deciding whether meetings are desirable, and if so, which is the most useful form for probationers; we shall return to this problem in the last chapter. Institutes have not always been successful in their efforts: 'Some years ago we tried to help these teachers by convening a series of meetings, but we found that the demand was spasmodic and the needs so various that we did not get very far. One of the most pressing problems of probationers is to reconcile what they have learned at their training college with practice and procedure required by the Heads of the schools in which they are teaching; but it is obvious that this is an embarrassing subject to discuss. I do know that the Local Authority Inspectors in this area give a good deal of help to probationary teachers, and possibly this is the best approach.' On the other hand, in the Birmingham enquiry the probationers rated help from the other probationers rather more highly than that from local inspectors and organisers. Opportunities for meetings of probationers would seem worthwhile, if only to give them a feeling of assistance at hand, although to a more experienced eye, the reality of help provided might seem small. As one Institute Secretary put it: 'In our experience the most pressing problems of probationers are raised by their own unawareness of problems!' Be that as it may, it is clear that while Institutes are anxious to help, the form of help needed is by no means clear. The situation is further complicated because many probationers are miles from an Institute.

Some L.E.A.'s—the minority—make contact with local

colleges, but mostly in terms of reference back for individual probationers who do not happen to be doing well. A few colleges have reported having weekend conferences for their former students, and these provide a feed-back of information about the suitability of their training courses as well as an opportunity for discussion of probationary year experiences. But as with parent-teacher meetings, not all those former students whom one would particularly like to see, do, in fact turn up. This book is an attempt to make up in some way for their absence.

2

The first post

Obtaining a post

In the Spring *The Times Educational Supplement* begins to swell with portents of the future, advertisements for jobs in the schools. And even earlier than this L.E.A. officers have begun to interview students in their final year. L.E.A.'s with colleges nearby may see applicants in the colleges; and in fact one suggested cure for the teacher shortage in any area is to build a college of education within it, for some students, particularly men, like to settle near their college. Most local authorities, as do some schools, call applicants for interview. By April, authorities have begun to make offers of posts to potential teachers before, of course, they know exactly which posts will be vacant and before students have completed their training.

Authority appointments are mostly for posts in primary schools although they include some in secondary schools too. There is a wide variation between authorities not only in the number of appointments made centrally, i.e. not through schools, but also in the whole attitude towards appointments. There is no doubt that many students prefer appointments direct to individual schools. Most authorities who go in for mass appointments do try very quickly to place a student in a suitable school. They try to let students know about their future positions some time during the summer term, as posts become vacant. Nevertheless an

16

increasing number of college students, especially specialist secondary teachers, but including primary teachers, can and do apply for specific posts in schools; while for graduate teachers most of whom are specialists, the tendency has always been to apply to the particular schools. It is advantageous to schools too, if they can see and have some say in the choosing of their new colleagues. Some authorities are aware of this and one of the spokesmen said: 'A good Head for a probationer is one who has had some say in his appointment.'

The appointment to specific posts is easier for some authorities than others. Some cover many schools and there are those, that, through no fault of their own, have many 'difficult' schools and a shortage of staff. Here there is a great temptation to press-gang probationers into the schools which other teachers are hastily leaving. In these situations the newest recruit is being asked to do the most difficult job. However, the majority of authorities are able to keep probationers out of difficult schools. Unfortunately this majority includes many authorities where probationers are few. The areas where many probationers are absorbed, thickly populated, heavily industrialised zones, cannot do this; in reply to enquiries they said: 'usually' or 'we try to' or 'no, we cannot', keep probationers out of difficult schools.

Living at home or away

Actually many students are so anxious to teach near their homes, their spouses or their betrothed that this outweighs any other consideration. Their prime interest is in a locality, the educational opportunities are a secondary consideration. Often they can even choose specialist posts in a particular area: 31% of the Leicester probationers of 1961 and 1962 had succeeded in doing this. Naturally non-specialist posts are much easier to get and 70% of the Birmingham infant school probationers had managed to get posts at home. Some women students go home for a year as a kind of conscience saver, sandwiched between several years away at college or university and permanent departure to live with a husband. It is also easier to save money at home. Some men graduates go home to teach in a non-specialist post while looking around for a different profession. These two factors mean that probationers living at home include more birds of passage than one might expect.

Living at home appears to have certain hidden advantages. Those Leicester probationers who were living with their parents managed to keep well to a notably greater extent than those living in lodgings or flats. More of those teaching in junior and secondary modern schools lived at home—as one would expect—but for probationers teaching in all kinds of schools, the trend was the same. Home life seems to give some kind of support if only in the most obvious way of providing meals, a clean room, fresh laundry and a general feeling of being looked after on arriving home tired from school. Living with a husband or wife did not have these benefits and absence from school occurred as frequently among these teachers as among the unmarrieds living in lodgings or flats.

Financial worries are also alleviated by living with parents. Among the Birmingham probationers those living in 'digs' and flats complained most about financial difficulties. Probationers at the moment earn £800 per annum if college trained, £900 per annum if a graduate, untrained and without a 'good honours' degree, and £1,020 per annum if still untrained but with a 'good honours' degree. When a graduate trains he has an addition of £80 a year to the salaries just quoted, this extra £80 remains with him throughout his career. And £30 can be obtained for a

18

further year's study of any appropriate kind, up to a maximum of three years. There are a certain number of graded posts in schools carrying extra increments which, although rarely obtained by probationers, make life more opulent.

The education policy of L.E.A.'s

Living at home has many attractions for young teachers, but it may have certain unfortunate side effects too. It may encourage a probationer to teach in an area which, educationally speaking could be much better, or is just not suitable for his particular needs at that point in his career. Authorities vary in educational policy, the state of school buildings, percentage of pupils staying at school beyond fifteen years of age, the supply of part-time teachers, the extent of educational research going on in the area, freedom to allocate school funds, and so on. Even if the decision to take a post is largely geographically determined the probationer should also know where he stands educationally.

It is equally important that the school should know where the new probationer stands educationally also. Colleges (and departments) supply information about the strengths and weaknesses of their students to the local authorities; most supply teaching grades also. According to the N.U.T. and A.T.C.D.E. (1961, p. 4) 'It would appear that often this information (from college and department) is not transmitted by the authority to schools.' Dr. Edmonds (1967) has suggested that research might be directed towards the standardisation of grades and comments from different colleges so that they could be more easily used.

One of the difficulties is possibly that different authorities have individual standards themselves. It has already been mentioned that the proportion of probationers among the serving teachers varies very much from one authority to another and the proportion of new teachers who are not successful and have their probation extended varies with the authorities too. It was in 1961/62 for example, higher in counties than in county boroughs and higher in London than elsewhere.

The type of school post

The N.U.T. is concerned to develop a better introduction of new teachers to schools. In *Teachers in their First Posts* (1961, p. 5) it says: 'It is essential, however, that teachers taking up a first post should be informed in detail about that post at the earliest possible moment. They should have the opportunity of visiting the school well in advance of commencing their duties.' In some schools this does happen. In other cases, probationers find themselves in situations similar to that of the girl who in her first term, never knew what she was going to be asked to teach until she arrived at the school in the morning.

Usually probationers do know something of the school and their future work before the Autumn term begins. Threequarters of the Leicester probationers had visited their schools before the term started no matter whether they were to teach in junior, grammar, modern or comprehensive schools. The majority also knew something of their future timetables and syllabuses, but in this respect the students going into grammar schools were much better off than the rest. Of the secondary modern school probationers, 37% began to teach without being able to plan any of their work ahead, in total ignorance of both syllabuses and forms to be taught. This result was probably not due to the reluctant graduate teachers taking last minute jobs, for the Birmingham enquiry among nongraduates produced stories of similar and rather worse

20

experiences. Such lack of preparation by the schools gives no encouragement to new teachers to prepare their own work thoroughly and is guaranteed to exacerbate any feelings of insecurity which they may happen to have.

It is often suggested that probationers are given the classes that nobody else wants; backward streams and rowdy adolescents. Sometimes this is true: 'I had one difficult form—a bottom set of fourth year who had had about six teachers of maths, none of whom could control them.' But it should be noticed that even here it was just one form which was involved and, so far, there is no evidence to show, in any of the enquiries, that by and large probationers get an undue share of 'leavings'. They possibly do not get as many of the 'bright' forms as perhaps proportionately they should. It is also the case that, in some difficult secondary schools and some girls' schools, the proportion of probationers is so high that it is impossible to find enough good first and second year forms to go round.

There appear however certain almost traditional ways of settling in probationers. Infant teachers tend to be given the five-year-olds and in junior schools, the girls get the first forms while the men get the 9-year group. It seems to be assumed that the older children can be more easily managed by men, and that any omissions of a probationer can be more easily rectified the longer the children have in school after they have left the probationer's class. Of the new secondary school teachers some will indeed be spared the responsibility of a class but, of those who do, many will be given a first form, both teacher and taught, as in the primary schools, then being new. Secondary school probationers teach a large number of classes per week, most commonly some six to ten according to the Birmingham enquiry, and hence have many boys and girls to get to know. They are also expected to be flexible in their teaching methods, adapting themselves—or trying to—to work with the bright, rather bright, the dull and very dull. Graduates going into secondary schools sometimes obtain graded posts or posts of special responsibility, especially, of course, if they are scientists or mathematicians, and this means that they may have considerable administrative duties straightway. These probationers usually get no payment for this during the first year, but do so on completion of probation, except in the case of some modern schools. Responsibility without financial recognition was found more frequently in these schools. At least this was how it appeared to the new Leicester teachers; it usually meant that they were working on their own with full responsibility for their subject, but without extra pay.

Teaching commitments during the first year

Schools have different patterns of activities within them. It would be true to say that generally the younger the child the more the teacher's time is given to actively teaching a class and the less time there is free for marking, preparation and writing reports. The most common number of free periods per week among the Leicester junior school probationers was two—although one third had none—while in all three types of secondary schools it was five, with an occasional under-employed person in a modern or a grammar school with twelve or more. Nevertheless, the average for grammar schools was higher than that for modern because there were fewer teachers with less than five free periods in the grammar schools. The comprehensive schools came in between. There was no evidence that science teachers were favoured with more free periods.

To balance against lack of free time in a junior school there were fewer demands for non-teaching activities. For example, only one Leicester probationer out of thirty in junior schools had to write termly reports, whereas this applied to 22% of the modern, 32% of the comprehensive and 65% of the grammar school probationers. Report writing is ubiquitous these days, but it still flourishes most strongly in grammar schools.

There is also, I believe, a general expectation that the younger the average age of the children in the school, the less the preparation and marking required of the teacher in charge of them. Some direct evidence of this point was obtained by looking at the time which some Leicester probationers, in different types of schools, said they spent on marking and preparation. Thirty-four history and geography graduates teaching in modern schools were compared with thirty-four history and geography graduates teaching in grammar schools. On average the modern school teachers spent six hours on marking and six on preparation each week, while the grammar school teachers spent nine hours on preparation and seven on marking. It seems likely that in general, modern school probationers spend a shorter time on lesson preparation and perhaps on marking too, than do their counterparts in grammar schools; and modern school teachers spend longer than junior school teachers. A comparison was made between thirty graduates in modern schools, with the same subject and class of degree as the thirty graduates working in junior schools. Those in modern schools spent longer on marking and preparation than did those in junior schools.

Nevertheless a glance at individual records of probationers working in the same types of schools showed remarkable differences in the time which was given to keeping up with individual teaching commitments. Among the junior teachers, for example, some only spent two or three hours on marking and preparation each week while others spent up to twenty. Variation among the work done by secondary school teachers was even greater. Some spent as much as fifteen (and in one case twenty-four) hours per week marking, while preparation might absorb up to twenty hours. Others managed with three hours of marking and one or two hours of preparation. The two striking things about the probationers' time records were their wide variation and the exhausting length of some of them: many probationers must have been very tired.

Some of these differences will stem, of course, from the actual teaching demands of particular time-tables: a great range of forms, an unfamiliar historical period, unread set books, a non-special subject, no apparatus for a particular teaching method, unsure foundations of basic skills: 'I was amazed at my gaps of knowledge of comparative simple grammatical rules', and so on. And some will stem from minor compulsions of the probationers themselves, a desire for security in the insecurity of beginning a new job, or a wish not to be caught out by the children.

At the other extreme we have new teachers with too much confidence in themselves, or a lack of appreciation of the organisation involved in most lessons. Hypnotised by the off-hand approach of an experienced and highly successful teacher they leave far too much to the inspiration of the moment. They have too great a faith in exhaustible spontaneity, demanding that it quench the thirst of a thirty-period week for a twelve-week term. Such probationers invariably suffer from inspirational drought and need to be made to replenish themselves.

Duties and out-of-school activities of probationers

In addition to the giving and preparation of lessons probationers are of course engaged in duties, extra curricular activities and school visits. All these add to the probationer's physical and spiritual involvement in the school.

24

Some are much enjoyed but in some cases, 'extraneous duties' to quote the Birmingham survey do provide problems for the probationary year.

The names of some of the duties undertaken by Leicester probationers conjure up pictures of interesting school differences: 'house patrol', 'block supervision', 'corridor duty', presumably describe much the same activity; 'yard duty', 'playground supervision', 'break' and 'recess' are suggestive of quite different educational worlds; 'early morning', 'gate duty', 'assembly' and 'clearance' all describe by implication different ways of beginning and ending a school day. There are also puzzling differences in the length of time considered essential to carry out these duties. The ever present 'dinner duty' sometimes called 'dinner supervision' or rarely 'lunch', ranged from twenty minutes to one and a half hours each day, 'playground' could extend from twenty minutes to sixty and even 'milk supervision' spanned from ten minutes to forty.

The usual custom is for each member of staff to have a certain number of duties each week, e.g. 'corridor and playground duty one day a week for a whole year at break and dinner time', plus one or two detention supervisions thrown in as extras each term. Some schools, particularly boys' schools, go in for weekly marathons: 'All duties for a week' with a 'rest' for the remainder of the term. When due allowance has been made for this method of organising duties, it is apparent that, as with the lesson preparation there are wide differences in what probationers have to undertake. Approximately one fifth of the Leicester probationers had no duties at all (except a detention or so), while one tenth had four or more each week. The average number, in round figures for all probationers was two per week, with modern and junior schools showing a tendency to be just above and grammar schools just below this figure. Those probationers in small schools (one- or two-form entry) and those in large (five or more form entry) appeared to come off worst, with the exception of the modern schools. However, within schools of the same size, there was a considerable variation in the number of school duties.

Similarly, out of school, or extra-curricular activities seem to have absorbed the energies and enthusiasm of some probationers more than others: approximately 40% of probationers in junior schools, 60% in modern schools, 90% in comprehensive and 80% in grammar had been helping out with clubs or after school games in their first year. The clubs ranged from flower arrangement, radio, judo, table tennis and film club to the more usual debating society, young farmers' club, aero club, and such old stand-bys as the choir, dramatic society, Christian Union, Scouts and Guides and the rugby club. All secondary schools appear to be getting more 'club conscious' although these are still differences between types of schools. Educational holidays also are now organised for pupils and about 80 Leicester probationers had already taken part in these. In addition there are day expeditions to sports matches, theatres and places of educational interest. Again by far the majority of the probationers had helped in some way, the one exception being the junior school probationers; but they made up for this lack of participation in, for example, theatre visits (not unexpected) by being more completely engaged in parents meetings and the production of plays, one suspects of the inevitable, but perennially attractive, nativity plays.

The impression created is of a surprising amount of energetic participation in all sorts of school affairs and it is not true that what is lost in time on the swings of out-of-school activities is gained on the roundabouts of teaching responsibility. In the modern schools for example, those probationers with more frequent report writing were also more active in clubs. There were few complaints about this, however, and several probationers recommended participation in out of school activities as an especially good way of getting to know children and being accepted by them. Older staff might disagree. Sometimes it is difficult for the young teacher to change from the informal rôle of being club helper to the more formal rôle of class teacher or even to realise that such a change is required; but only one probationer admitted to experiencing difficulty of this sort.

The teacher's rôle—expectations of probationers and pupils

However this problem of change from club to class raises the question of how the probationer sees himself as a teacher, whether he sees himself as primarily concerned with passing on certain skills and knowledge or whether he sees himself as having wider responsibilities. In the nineteenth century many teachers were seen by society, if not by themselves, as missionaries bringing 'sweetness and light' to the humbler classes—from which they themselves had come and to which they would return.

At present this aspect of the teacher's rôle may be said to have survived in the idea of a teacher-social worker and, at a more sophisticated level in Floud's (1962, p. 304) notion of a 'crusader in the suburb', 'dedicated to the war against mediocrity and to the search for excellence'. Some probationers certainly see themselves in one or other of these dual rôles. They wish not only to teach their pupils but to rescue them either from intellectual or material poverty.

There is a move to educate teachers and social workers together, to deal with the many latch-key children, whose mothers go out to work, found on large housing estates built to relieve the substandard housing problems. These children present a new teacher—to quote a Leicester graduate—with 'not only a problem in education but a fairly serious social problem.' These are the schools which especially require a teacher with the dual rôle of teacher-social worker. It is a moot point whether probationers should ever go into these schools, perhaps irrelevant at the moment because, in fact, they do. These are the schools which are difficult to staff and hence wait open-doored for probationers. And these are the schools where middle-class assumptions about academic learning and general behaviour are brought sharply into question. The expectations of probationers going into them should be different, those of the children certainly will be. Probationers should carefully consider whether they wish and are suitably prepared, to go into these schools. L.E.A.'s should give very special care to young teachers whom they send into the 'Educational priority areas' of the *Plowden Report* (1967).

The children themselves have views on what they want a teacher to be. This is how one probationer saw the expectations of her junior school children and how these expectations should be met:

> They will look to you for guidance in many things, even little things like packing desks quietly. Tell them right on your first day how you want them to do *everything*. Don't be discouraged at first if it seems overwhelming. Enjoy the children: listen to all their news, laugh at their jokes, share their fun.

The accent is on 'their'. Another probationer saw the children's expectations about her very differently: 'Don't go to be a friend to the children, they regard you as an enemy.' These are, of course, children's concepts of a teacher, through the eyes of the teacher.

There are however, a few researches into what children themselves say a good teacher should be. On the whole their ideas have a slightly old-fashioned air: Taylor (1962, p. 264) found that 'children in general evaluate most highly the good teacher's teaching'; they expect, if you like, a professional job, well done. It is only among adolescents that a good teacher's personal qualities, particularly his cheerfulness, good temper and sense of humour are much appreciated, possibly because adolescents' rebellion tests out these qualities and often finds them wanting. Nevertheless, even here, adolescents in some schools evaluate teachers for their cleverness and knowledge. But they do not, according to Wright (1961, pp. 226-232) value them as highly as persons. Obviously there is a lack of subtlety in a pupil's appraisal or appreciation of what is involved in teaching, of what in fact makes a teacher 'good', but it is equally obvious that pupils also come to the class room of the probationer armed with definite expectations about what a teacher should be and what a teacher should do. There is sometimes disappointment all round, as well as unexpected pleasant surprises.

Achievement during the probationary year

In general, despite some horrifying social problems, unrealistic expectations, endless names to learn, duties to do, lessons to prepare, books to mark, field trips to make, games to umpire, plays to produce, parents meetings to attend, reports to write and last, but by no means least, lessons to give, the majority of probationers enjoy their first year. Some Leicester probationers enjoyed 'all of it', 'every minute of it'. While this continuous bliss is rare, the majority of the Aberdeen probationers (and the Manchester young teachers), 60% in fact, found teaching 'as satisfactory as expected'. In the Manchester survey (Rudd and Wiseman, 1962), the infant school teachers and the grammar school masters were the most generally satisfied, although this enquiry, it must be remembered, relates to teachers who had been in school for five years and began their probation in 1955.

Another way of getting some measure of probationers' performances in schools is to compare how they taught as students with how they managed as school teachers. In the very few British enquiries so far (Tudhope, 1942; Collins, 1959; Pearce, 1959), a positive and significant correlation has been found between teaching grades given to students in teaching practice and assessment of their teaching during the early years of teaching, whether the assessment has been made by Heads of schools, H.M.I.'s or tutors. Except in one instance the correlations have been rather low which means that many probationers have done much worse or much better than their training grades would have indicated. Improvement is usually related to finding a reasonable school which differs markedly in character from the one in which the original failure occurred. Progress is also associated with the alleviation of personal problems and an improvement in health (Collins, 1958).

L.E.A.'s are informed when a student qualifies with a 'D' teaching mark and advisers usually visit these former weak students more frequently; they often place them in specially selected schools. One Authority in the Leicester enquiry, usually kept 'D' probationers out of the quota and treated the new teachers more as students as far as responsibilities went. However, this kind of special help for probationers about to make a shaky start cannot be counted on: 28 L.E.A.'s said they had no special provision for 'D' teachers. Sometimes, of course, a good student develops unexpected weaknesses on probation: among the Aberdeen probationers for example, two 'A' college teachers were given 'D' grades by H.M.I.'s, but this is very exceptional.

If, at the end of the year in England or Wales, the probationer is still teaching badly, he, as mentioned in Chapter 1, may have the probationary period extended for six months or more, or he may in very rare cases, be advised to leave teaching. Most probationers improve sufficiently during the period of extension to be acceptable as a teacher to the local authority and hence to the Department of Education and Science. In cases of extended probation, Heads of schools may help in various ways; by giving more assistance with lesson preparation; by arranging perhaps for speech therapy if this has a chance of helping either directly, or indirectly; by introducing more games into the probationer's time-table to provide experience of enforcing rules where enforcement is generally easier. A few L.E.A.'s get in contact with the probationer's college or department. Some L.E.A.'s encourage probationers with difficulties to visit other schools; a few have special courses.

The most general way of giving help, other than by additional visits of advisers, is to provide an opportunity for the probationer to transfer to another school. But prevention is better than cure and much can be, and often is, done by careful placement when the probationer begins teaching. Probationers might help themselves more than they do by not being homebound, by applying to areas where schools are likely to be more suitable to them.

Many teachers who manage to complete their probationary year quite satisfactorily do themselves, however, have strong doubts during the year. This happens most frequently in those schools with which the probationers are least familiar, such as comprehensive schools.

This brings up the question of how far teaching practice prepares the student for the job he is going to take. One L.E.A. Officer said: 'Many teachers are trained to think in terms of teaching groups of approximately 30 children of the same age. In rural areas this situation is not common.' Obviously it is impossible to prepare for all exigencies but it should not be possible for a junior school probationer to begin her job without some knowledge of infant methods. Possibly some departments and colleges are better at preparing students for one type of school rather than others. One probationer scoffed at the idea of precise preparation, 'No school is like any other school. The most valuable lesson is adaptability'—obviously a successful probationer! But not all new teachers are so versatile or so able to take things easily in their stride; some get worried, tired and ill. They should have been given better preparation and chosen their school more carefully.

One third of the Aberdeen probationers said that they had found teaching a strain on the health, although only 12% had been absent from school for ten days or more during the two year probation. Among the Leicester probationers, with the exception of the trained graduates teaching in grammar schools, 38% had been away from school for at least one day during the first year; only 26% of the trained graduates in grammar schools had been absent. The absences were due to all kinds of illnesses, including, as one would expect, a large number of throat infections, sixteen cases of tonsilitis, twenty-one of laryngitis and pharyngitis, and many bouts of colds and bronchitis. Other types of illnesses included eight cases of migraine and nervous troubles, several cases of measles, but few other infectious diseases. One student, who had had two attacks of 'flu, added with a melancholy implication, that he had 'lost weight slightly since student days'. Another commented 'six days with 'flu, my first illness since the age of five!' While a third described a not uncommon experience when he said 'felt at a low ebb physically but never away'.

In the joint recommendations of the N.U.T. and the

A.T.C.D.E. (1961) it suggests that a Working Party should consider the health of teachers during the probationary year and this certainly seems necessary. Absences from school would seem to be the result of certain strains: those probationers in more 'protected' situations such as trained graduates in grammar schools and those living with parents were the ones with fewer absences from school. No doubt there is greater inducement to stay away from some schools than others. Nevertheless, when we consider the school activities in which many probationers take part, it is not surprising that the physical and mental wear and tear takes its toll.

True some probationers with, superficially, the same kind of job, work harder than others—as we have already noticed. Some might be described as born workers. There was some evidence from the Leicester probationers that a proportion of those who worked hardest during the first year tended to work harder than ever in the second, and the extra work was not due entirely to promotions. In any case over half of the probationers said that they worked harder during their first year of teaching than they did as undergraduates.

In these days of shortage of teachers, probationers can, if they find one job too hard, try another elsewhere, but many have the feeling that, unless marriage intervenes, there is a certain commitment to a school for two years at least. Others stay, not from a sense of loyalty, but for other reasons: 'purely for reference purposes. It is a bad school' or for the benefit of a 'second chance', or to stay 'with an identical class to improve on last year'. In fact among the Leicester teachers 78% of those in junior, modern and comprehensive schools continued to teach in the same school for a second year, while in the grammar schools this applied to 90%. Those who left their schools were not always anxious to depart; as one said, 'Would

33

have been happy to stay but left owing to marriage'. Among the Aberdeen probationers (in a variety of schools) 22% had left their first school by the end of two years probationary period. But of course, in the enquiries about past students, those who never reply probably contain a high proportion who have left their posts, and these are not included in the statistics. This may give an over optimistic picture of the real situation. Nevertheless, it is clear that many students had enjoyed their first posts and had remained in them for a second year.

3

Heads and colleagues

Expectations about Heads in schools

It has been said that the English stand up for God, The
Queen and Headmasters. Godlike qualities are certainly
ascribed by some probationers to their Heads: 'A very
strong Headmistress who had the habit of being every-
where at once. The ability to hear the slightest whisper—
see through closed doors.' All-seeing and all-knowing, this
is what some teachers are expecting their Heads to be, and
they are very disappointed when they turn out to be all
too weakly human after all. 'Girls had no respect for the
Headmistress, and the staff despaired of taking further
action on their own.' Obviously, the Head was seen by
these Leicester probationers as the lynch pin of the whole
school structure. Irrational as well as rational demands
are made on Heads.

Actually, as we have noted in Chapter 1 the role played
by the Head in relation to probationers varies with the
type of school. In junior schools, he tends to be all things
to all probationers; he is paternalistic in his attitude. In
modern and grammar schools, the paternalism continues,
but the activities of 'the old man' are much more
restricted. In a strange way, the relationship between the
Head and his staff seems to be influenced by the age of
the pupils; it mirrors the pattern of behaviour appropriate
to them. The relationship changes as the *pupils* grow older.

Comprehensive schools seem to differ; and a new pattern appears to be emerging. The Head is seen as primarily an administrator, a 'grey eminence' behind the teachers' first year.

Some young teachers, but not many, are aware of the unrealistic expectations which haunt some schools. As one said, 'Headmasters are administrators, too. Expediency counts with some. Don't expect to work with an educational paragon.' The school is an institution particularly vulnerable to the development of irrational feelings. It has much of the organisation of an extended family, and this means that ways of behaving, thinking and feeling developed within young teachers' own families are very easily projected into it. Members of the community come to stand all too easily for much hated or well-loved family figures, grandparents, aunts, uncles, mother and father, brothers and sisters. The new teacher may feel extraordinarily dependent and unable to take the initiative in this environment so richly evocative of family situations where dependency was appropriate and encouraged. Indeed, some probationers may feel a great strain in a school when this dependency need is not met : 'The Headmaster believed in each member of staff maintaining personal discipline; and this hinders inexperienced teachers; their work becomes duller than it should be, because they spend too much thought on keeping forms in hand.' Basic needs cannot be eliminated simply by making no provision for them, however undesirable these needs may be.

Another factor which may befog a probationer's initial relation with the Head of the school is the type of organisation experienced in college. If the organisation there was very free and democratic, with the Principal easily approachable, and the probationer finds himself in a school run on closely guided lines with an authoritarian Head, then there are likely to be major difficulties of adjustment

36

for the probationer. There are likely to be difficulties in such apparently simple procedures as how to get in to see the Head in the first place and, once inside, how to talk to him about important matters. If the contrary situation has prevailed in college, the probationer has been used to a good deal of guidance from an authoritarian Principal, then a democratic Head may appear a broken reed.

Several L.E.A.'s, when asked which type of Head, in their experience, was best for probationers, said that it was the Head who worked as leader of a team, and made the new teacher feel part of a team. C. Sofer, when talking about business institutions in *The Organisation from Within*, says (p. 168) that 'there is little doubt that organisation functions best when leaders lead'. There are, however, different ways of leading. Some Heads, well aware of their own limitations, or—a rather dangerous situation this —still esentially dependent themselves, or as a matter of principle, recoil from direct leadership. This is all to the good if the reasons and feelings for it are understood and the expectations of the school staff not too openly flaunted, but, again according to Sofer, participative leadership may, in some cases, be an abdication of leadership. Obviously there are good and bad cases of authoritarian and of democratic leadership, and one type of leadership may be more suited to one probationer rather than to another. But in both cases the Head must be prepared to respect his staff, and to shoulder his responsibilities. No probationer could thrive in a school where 'The Headmaster frequently countermanded staff orders to pupils; often dressed down staff in front of pupils. When I arrived, there had been no staff meeting for four years.'

The Head of a school must be able to accept responsibility both for what might be described as the objective demands of the school, and for some of the unadmitted emotional needs of the community. Sofer makes this point

37

in a rather different way: he says (p. 169) that 'Although the staff will not respect a leadership which permits an inefficient organisation, they will sabotage one that neglects the needs of its members'. No probationer should have to join a school engrossed in take-over bids and palace revolutions.

Many probationers, of course, begin teaching in schools with 'inefficient organisations'. We have already seen that secondary modern schools tend to be particularly unprepared to give sufficient forethought to allocation of timetables. This reflects, in a curious way, the hand to mouth existence of the working-class neighbourhood in which many of these schools exist.

This inefficient organisation is also related to the concept of the rôle of the Head as a side-line occupation. He is, after all, the Head 'teacher', the Head 'master' and not the manager, the director or the principal. He is, as others are, primarily a teacher, and he fits in other activities including school organisation, as best he may. Except in very small schools, this is not, however, a realistic view of the rôle of Head. There is lack of due recognition, often by the Head himself, of his rôle as a policy maker and co-ordinator of the work of the teachers in his school. This aspect of leadership falls most hardly on the Heads of modern schools, for they have the least help from tradition, and from the inevitability imposed by external examining boards.

A further demand made upon Heads of many schools at the moment, is that they should act as a link between one group of teachers and the next. The change-over of staff is so great in some schools that, whereas formerly a new teacher could be easily absorbed into the school community, today this is often not so, and special arrangements are needed in order to ensure that information is provided and a welcome given. This can, to some extent, make up for the absence of a stable staff community, the loss of which is generally recognised. To quote one L.E.A. official: 'A major difficulty is that many schools no longer have a sound core of experienced teachers who between them establish and maintain a good disciplinary tone for the whole school, creating a general atmosphere which is of great value to the beginner, who is probably unconscious of its existence, although enjoying its benefits.' More than ever before, forethought and dissemination of information seem necessary.

Expectation of Heads about probationers

So far, we have considered the Head's rôle from the point of view of the newcomer to the school—what the Head can be expected to do for him. Naturally the Head has expectations too. Some of these reflect personality differences among Heads. Compare, for example, the attitudes of these two Heads to an apparently similar situation: one said, 'their [i.e. probationers'] vocation is teaching children, *not* a subject. Too many thought of teaching as a means of bettering themselves—not the pupils, e.g. must have 'A' level, then I can get a graded post', and the other wrote, 'He is (staying on) but is understandably seeking a post in which he can teach the subject at a higher level, and can also apply for a responsibility allowance in due course'. The latter has obvious attributes of sympathy and understanding; he can identify with the probationer, but perhaps identifies too little with his own school. The former's concern for individuals is limited to his children, and excludes the probationer, whom he does not individualise at all; instead, he talks about '*their* reaction', and 'bettering *themselves*'.

These two quotations are taken from replies from Heads of schools in which the Leicester probationers were working. Many showed strikingly different points of view. Several commented, with approval, on probationers' 'ideas' and 'infectious enthusiasms'; others objected to 'half-baked notions'. Some saw their new teachers in terms of how well they wrote on the blackboard; how well, or ill, they dealt with registers, mark sheets, etc.: 'he lacked necessary classroom manners and was lost in school administration'. Others were impressed by out-of-school activities; 'a willingness to be more than a 9-4 man'.

Just as we have seen that probationers in different types of schools expected different things of their Heads, so we may see there are school differences also in the expectations of the Heads about their probationers. For instance, a probationer's confidence and poise was more often remarked upon by grammar school Heads, and yet one would have thought that this would be a valuable characteristic in any type of school. Again, teaching skills would seem worthy of comment in all kinds of schools, but in fact this turned out not to be so. They were most obviously in the minds of Heads of junior, modern and comprehensive schools. Similarly, all schools provide a community of colleagues with which the probationers are intimately concerned, and yet it was the grammar schools only which considered this of prime importance: 'he fitted into the staff room well'; 'he was a good and loyal colleague'.

The differences, while undoubtedly related to personal differences among the probationers themselves, owed a good deal to differences among the Heads, some due to personality differences, but others due, as we have noticed to different school expectations.

The dual rôle of the Head in relation to probationers

Heads, as was mentioned in Chapter 1, have to report to

L.E.A.'s on the progress of probationers in their schools. Some probationers are unaware of this, while others certainly know because the reports are read out to them. In the latter situation, the Head is following a suggestion of the N.U.T. that no reports on a teacher should be given without the former being aware of it; to act otherwise is to be guilty of unprofessional conduct. Some Heads get over what might be a conflict between the demands of professional conduct and the sensitivity of the probationer by telling him the contents of the report without actually reading it out to him. In this way, if some hard words are required in the report, an opportunity is given to smooth away some of the cutting edges by a general explanation. Other Heads seem to keep the probationer in the dark about the whole procedure, and no comment whatsoever is made, so that in the end the probationer can only deduce that no news is good news, and that he has passed his probationary year.

This openly stated, or inwardly implied, concern of the Head with the new teacher's successful completion of probation, means that a Head has two special relationships with his probationer—one concerned with assessing him as a teacher and the other concerned with helping him during the probationary year. In Chapter 1 we noticed that L.E.A. officials also play a similar dual rôle. It needs little imagination to see that these rôles may conflict. One would think twice about going to a Head with a problem which might be counted as a mark of failure, or of putting forward the claims of a new method of teaching contrary to the views forcefully expressed by the Head. There would be a tendency to play safe, so that new techniques would not be tried out, or old problems would be kept well in the background.

The comments of the Heads about students in the Leicester enquiry did not indicate that they were aware of this dual rôle problem, possibly because, to them, there was so little question of the probationer 'failing'. Virtually all probationers pass. But if the Heads were unaware of the problem, it was clear from the probationers' comments, in the same enquiry, that they were alive to the difficulties.

Many probationers solved the problem by dividing the rôles and transferring one elsewhere; they asked the staff for help and left the assessment to the Head. A few got out of difficulty by deliberately pretending that no help was needed: 'Give the appearance of being able to cope. Not to worry about low standard of work and behaviour and stealing of school property'; in other words, don't let on. But on the whole, in most schools, the Head seemed to take the initiative in giving help, and in fact, according to the Birmingham survey, the Head often thinks that he is being more helpful than the probationer feels to be so.

Actually, the helping rôle alone has difficulties within itself. Most Heads, particularly those in junior schools, take their helping rôle seriously. Some demand detailed preparation of lessons and the keeping of records. To some probationers this may appear as an irksome continuance of college supervision. But the Head may have a real difficulty in getting information on which to base his advice, and then having got the information, there still remains the problem of how to give the advice without destroying the confidence and authority of the probationer. Secondary schools Heads of departments and L.E.A. officials have, of course, today, the same problem. Fifty years ago, and in some schools still, it would not be recognised as a problem. A probationer can still be disturbed by 'the Head's frequent visits, well intentioned but unnerving experiences'.

Yet what is a Head to do? Some L.E.A. officials and Heads give demonstration lessons. These may be quite acceptable if given in another school or in the same school when the general prestige of the new teacher is high, but are of doubtful value when conditions are bad and help most needed. The less formal approach of group work demonstration may be acceptable and very useful to an unsure probationer. However, even here much depends on whether the Head is generally around and what his approach to the children and staff happens to be. Revans (1964) found in his enquiry into hospital morale that there was a relationship between the attitude of the sister to the probationer in her charge and the way she saw the attitudes of her superiors to her; if she saw them as helpful, then she was helpful too. It seems likely that by and large a similar situation occurs in schools. The Head picks up his attitude from how he sees the L.E.A. officials' attitude to him. If he perceives his own treatment as good, then he is likely to treat his own probationers similarly, both in helping them and assessing their work.

Colleagues in the staff room

We have already commented on how the Heads of grammar schools attach more importance than do other Heads to the relationship which a probationer has with his colleagues. This difference probably stems from the position of forty or fifty years ago when both time and place for such relationships were lacking in other types of schools. Indeed even now they are often fewer than in grammar schools. Some of the Leicester junior school probationers had no free periods, and in 1966 there were still 7,463 primary schools without staff rooms (Central Advisory Council for Education p. 392). Nevertheless, the situation has much improved and continues to do so. There are also, as we have seen, many out-of-school activities of one kind or another found in schools. These give a further opportunity for the growth of friendly feelings, not only between staff and pupils, but between staff and staff. As Bryan Wilson (1962, p. 26) says in writing about the teacher's rôle, 'Affection needs activities and commitments on which to grow'.

These activities are hardly likely to flourish in a school such as this: 'Staff room downright lousy—21 men in a room smaller than my bed-sitting room'. It is true, as one colleague stated that 'The Spirit of the school (is) more important than its amenities', but there seems a level below which the physical standards must not fall. Given these, it seems that poor school buildings and inadequate facilities may play a useful rôle in channelling off some of the frustrations and aggression of the new teacher. One can grumble interminably about hard chairs and dirty walls and no feelings are hurt; they act as non-retaliatory scapegoats. In the Birmingham survey Head teachers mentioned probationers' problems with backward children, discipline and teaching methods more frequently than did the probationers actually involved in these situations. The probationers wrote instead of the inadequate buildings, poor equipment and few books.

Too liberal staff accommodation, while an architect's pride, may also, as one probationer noticed, be destructive of friendly staff relationships. In his school the staff rooms for different houses and departments were so large that 'every group or level was encouraged to stick to itself'. It seems unlikely that sufficient thought has been given to the problem of providing in schools opportunities both for isolation and for the coming together of various staff sub-groups.

It is often easier for probationers to begin in a small group, a somewhat isolated science department, a small infant school, or a house unit, and later to have the opportunity of widening contacts elsewhere, either in a much frequented common room of a large school or in a Teachers' club.

There are of course limitations on staff room relationships in addition to those provided by lack of physical facilities. For example, the new teacher is not going to get very far in this school: 'with two or three exceptions, the staff had left five minutes after the final bell—the Headmistress being the first to leave.' Nor will he progress in the school where there are all sorts of psychological limitations: where certain topics of conversation are taboo; where one cannot talk about the group work being tried out because group work is 'never done'; where the idea for the autumn mural is unmentionable because it might be copied by colleagues.

In the Leicester survey, the probationers in modern schools appeared to get least pleasure from their colleagues, while those in comprehensive schools most enjoyed their company. Some probationers are deeply disturbed by older teachers: one probationer advised a possible newcomer to his school to 'Take no notice of staff who crab everything one tries'. Another said, 'Develop a thick skin to old-fashioned criticism'. Undoubtedly not all difficulties arise from the colleagues: some come from the probationers themselves.

One situation with which the probationer has to come to terms is the discovery that he and many of his colleagues with whom he has to be in very close contact, think on very different lines. In a college or university, it is possible to be less aware of the differences between people. A large choice of friends is available and, as university life proceeds, friends come nearer together in common attitudes and interests. After the completion of the course, this enclosing world of group ideas and feelings disintegrates as members take up different jobs. It takes time for the isolated individual to adjust to the loss of this

support of understood and accepted opinion. It is a shock
for a former student who is permissive in outlook, and
who has, without thinking, mostly been friendly with like-
minded individuals, to find that his colleagues are 'solidly
authoritarian in sentiment'. He may be appalled to find
there are people who 'actually believe in flogging and hang-
ing and that these people are one's colleagues—one works
with them every day, meets them on N.U.T. committees'.

It is immature not to be prepared for differences of
opinion and attitudes of this kind, and one might argue
that to be cocooned in a university or college for three or
four years underlies this immaturity. Be that as it may,
former students are often shocked by the opinion of some
of the staff, particularly the older staff. One probationer
put as his greatest difficulty 'coming to terms with a hard
and cynical head of department'. This difference between
the old and the young is endemic in our society; in schools
it is brought sharply into focus for the probationers by the
confines of the staff room, and the sudden change—for
them—from a predominantly young group to one ap-
proaching middle age.

Fortunately, to set against these 'ghastly staff room
relationships', as one Leicester probationer described them,
there were many more of a helpful and satisfying kind.
Colleagues ranked second as the main source of pleasure:
'The Staff are as helpful and friendly as can be'. One probationer described his staff room as consisting of 'basically
happy and contented and progressive teachers (i.e. no
fellow travellers)!' Another urged a new colleague to 'Take
an active part in staff discussion'. Several remarked about
the congenial atmosphere of their staff rooms.

Probationers may, or may not—as we have remarked—
be acceptable colleagues themselves. Some people make
friends more easily than others, put up fewer defences, are
more thoughtful and sensitive; others have a natural wit

46

or charm. In the Leicester enquiry, those who said that they found making friends with their colleagues rather difficult also tended to find it more difficult to make friends in the community outside. This might suggest that part of the staff room problem was their own personal problem. In grammar schools, those who were married or living with parents found it easier to be friendly with colleagues, while in the other three types of school it was the unmarried probationer who most frequently had easy relationships.

Staff relationships are not only tremendously important in their own right, as a source of happiness and help, but they are also important in that they indirectly influence staff-pupil relationships. Attitudes are reflected and carried over into other situations, as we have already mentioned when discussing the Head/probationer relationship. Consider, for example, the comment of this probationer, intended as advice to a new colleague: '(1) Be very polite to senior staff (speak when you are spoken to, not otherwise), (2) Show the children you are boss from the word go, (3) Prepare your lessons well'. The last piece of advice shows the probationer to be conscientious and sensible, but a comparison of comments one and two shows a duplication of the attitude of senior staff to him in his own attitude to the children, of which, of course, he was completely unaware.

It is rarely possible for a new probationer to know much of the staff room attitude before he takes over the new job. If he finds the staff room uncongenial this may be largely the fault of his new colleagues or the fault may be within himself. He can only find this out by carefully considering the whole situation both in school and without. Or he might move to another school as this probationer did: 'I was very disillusioned by the staff who, I felt, were not interested in learning really. There were no out-of-

47

school activities. I moved at the end of the year. Delighted at the change.'

The problem of younger and older teachers

Wherever the probationer moves he is likely to have to live and work with much older colleagues. The new probationer has come from a college or university where he was a member of a majority group of youth. At the very least he will have to try out new social approaches, for likely as not, he has had no practice in relating closely to a group of this kind, where people of obviously different ages are doing superficially the same kind of job. In this situation, it is small things which mark off the years of experience. Trivial things often have a high significance; a special chair, the first cup of tea. But to the young teacher with his mind on the present, the customs may seem irritating and preposterous. The irritation may also be fed from unconscious sources. The relationships to older members of the staff may have a certain mother-in-law quality. In fact acceptance into a school is rather like acceptance into a new family. There are family customs to be learnt and however warm the welcome, a grain of jealousy between the newcomer and the established family group has to be dealt with. There is also an unacknowledged fear among the young of seeing themselves as they will be thirty years on. No one likes to grow old.

For these and other reasons, older members of staff are often a great threat to probationers and cause a good deal of unhappiness: 'Don't be afraid of older members of staff', 'Treat your senior colleagues with diffidence at first'. 'Do not be upset by the ignorance and boorishness of the older inhabitants' was another piece of advice, indicative of boorishness not only of the old, but of the young too.

Many probationers, being more sympathetic, or more

48

imaginative, or having older colleagues with these qualities, tackled the problem tactfully : 'Say little about the ideals and education which you learnt in training and listen to what the older staff say. Gradually introduce your new ideas.' It was the profound distrust and cynicism towards these new ideas which many students found so disturbing. Some of this undoubtedly was a projection on to older members of the probationer's own distrust in himself and his own ideas. A cynical staff room may provide a good excuse for not putting one's ideas to the test. Nevertheless this was not the whole truth.

Probationers themselves are, in turn, often unaware of the threat their youth and new ideas can be to older members of staff. Their own inner feelings of uncertainty prevent them from appreciating that they can be seen as a threat to anyone else. And yet, of course, they are; new methods may serve to remind senior staff how long ago their training was, and how their own teaching skills are being brought into question. The youth of the probationer attracts the children towards him even if outwardly they are rebelling. Hence with the affection of the children displaced and his teaching brought into question, the defensive reaction of the older member of staff can be all too easily one of cynicism and withdrawal. It is important that the probationer and his older colleagues should understand this dilemma; each constituting a threat to the other. Some young teachers are aware that they do not do all that they might to overcome initial uneasiness. As one young teacher said, 'Head of Department unapproachable, but if I had shown more initiative I could possibly have overcome this'.

Some probationers demand superhuman qualities from their older colleagues; while not looking too closely at their own. One untrained science graduate who had immediately acquired a teaching post carrying a special responsibility allowance, expressed great surprise at 'having to cope with members of staff being very bitter towards a very young Head of Department', not realising that some jealousy and bitterness were inevitable in this situation.

Cynicism is not a prerogative of older teachers. It can be found among the young: 'don't swamp yourself with work—play it cool'. The young may be condescending towards the old. Probationers often express disappointment with the level of staff room conversation, and yet at the same time do little to make it sparkle. This is partly due to the fact that they have, as has already been mentioned, lost their verbal sparring partners. They also—some of them—tend to become very dependent in the school situation, and do not feel it incumbent upon them to make the first move. Nevertheless, in some schools it would not be appreciated if they did; and this is a loss to all concerned.

Graduate and non-graduate colleagues

There is no doubt that there are difficulties sometimes when graduates and non-graduates work together on the same staff. This was brought out clearly in a discussion between probationers who had returned to their college for a week-end conference on the probationary year. One, a very confident-looking young man, said, 'The teachers in our school are worried about going comprehensive because they will be mixed up with graduate teachers who will be so much cleverer'. The new graduate teachers do not see it that way: they are usually over-awed by the training college probationers' 'know-how' and feel frustrated that their superior knowledge seems to aid them so little in putting it across.

There are obvious points of conflict here, between probationers with different backgrounds of training, different

scales of pay and different possibilities of promotion. As
one non-graduate teacher put it, 'let's face it we have two
classes of teachers, grammar and comprehensive' (Nicholson, 1965). Although one might draw the dividing line
rather differently, one would agree with the general meaning of the statement, the implications of which are rarely
discussed. Sometimes the difficulties are quietly dealt with
by stressing the contribution which non-graduates can
make to out-of-school activities. Obviously there is a problem of unity at a local level, within each staff room, and
at a national level in the profession as a whole.

School buildings and organisation and staff relationships

We have already suggested that the organisation of the
buildings of a school, the presence of separate science
buildings for example, or the absence of a staff room, can
make a good deal of difference to the ease or difficulty in
making friendships and sharing interests with colleagues.
The position of a room can also convey the value given
within the school to certain school activities. This was
brought out clearly in an instance reported in Joyce
Morris's book on *Standards and Progress in Reading* : one
primary school Head had her room, not in the junior
school section which is the more usual place, but in the
infant school buildings, indicating the over-riding importance which she attached to the introductory stages of
learning and the teachers concerned with it.

The common position of the Head's room, near to the
entrance of the school, exemplifies well the rôle of the
Head as the go-between, connecting the school with the
outside world. A Head's room tucked away at the top of
the stairs or at the end of a corridor attempts to deny the
necessity of this relationship. The Head's private study,
his personal cloakroom and his secretary's office all serve

to indicate a degree of separateness expected of most Heads. The isolation serves to give a certain charismatic quality to his person, but it also fosters all sorts of projections upon him, so that he may easily become the scapegoat of the rest of the staff. The vaguer the knowledge, the easier it is to make facts fit wishes. Indeed, the scapegoating of the Head may be—and sometimes is—a seemingly happy solution to staff room difficulties. The staff, and sometimes the pupils too, are united against a common enemy. But the Head is partially destroyed.

The isolation of the Head is a completely different matter from the physical isolation of a new teacher hidden away in the village hall, or in some temporary building at the bottom of the playground. Here, the young teacher may all too easily develop a strange feeling of not really belonging to the school, of isolation, a lack of worth. Actually a certain sense of isolation descends on probationers in any classroom, for the young teacher is alone, completely responsible for his own class, the only adult within speaking distance. In a way, a teacher leads a lonely professional life. This takes time to adjust to after the ubiquitous peer-group environment of college and university. Possibly open-plan teaching (such as that proposed for the new High Schools in Leicestershire), and team-teaching may make it easier for probationary teachers to begin their career.

Teachers at the moment do not meet as often as they might, or should, although more and more Heads are realising that Christmas parties and summer picnics for the staff and their wives, or husbands, are not only pleasant in themselves, but also help to promote good morale. To quote Josephine Klein (1961, p. 104), and to use sociological terms: 'a certain amount of expressive interaction is necessary for good morale.'

Working together over problems and having a say in

decision-making are even more effective means of bringing about active staff relationships—though not always of
a pleasurable kind! The young Birmingham teachers did
not rate staff meetings very highly as a means of helping
them with their job, but, in fact, the repercussion of a
judicious number of staff meetings is not likely to be
obvious to a beginner, while the harmful effects of none,
and the frustration of too many, may well be. Frequently,
the presence of staff meetings is taken to be indicative of
a democratic organisation in a school, but this may not be
so. A staff meeting may serve merely as a means of providing an audience to receive the Head's views, or an occasion
for a rebellious staff to erect a mob rule. An apparently authoritarian Head may consult his staff informally
on many occasions, and modify his ideas accordingly. In
our culture, 'democratic' or 'authoritarian' are emotive
words: to be democratic is to be approved, to be authoritarian is to be, at the very least, suspect. But from the
point of view of the *probationer* in a new school, the type
of organisation may be immaterial; what matters is the
quality of thought for the individual expressed in school
organisation. Revans (1964) found that in hospitals an
authoritarian attitude did not exclude good relationships
and guidance to new nurses.

The attitudes of the probationers within a school may
very quickly be picked up from colleagues. Colleges are
sometimes surprised at the changes which they see, or
hear of, in their former students during the first year's
teaching. But a very rapid introjection of other people's
feelings, of making them one's own in the school situation
was recorded in an investigation of Moeller and Charters
(1965), in the United States. They were interested in the
'sense of power' which teachers had in two different kinds
of administrative areas.

To their surprise the teachers had more sense of power,

felt more able to influence school policy and decide on their own work, in the area with the highly bureaucratic system, where their actual power was less. They had taken into themselves the power actually residing in the officials above them. In a similar way a probationer may have a great sense of authority in a tightly structured school where the Head's word is law. A probationer may find it a strain to exert his own individuality and authority in a class if he sees no exertion of authority by the Head of the school.

Schools, like other organisations, have formal and informal structures. To take the formal structure first, this consists of the Head, Deputy Head, Heads of departments, other teachers, school secretary and school caretaker, etc., all with their responsibilities and authority. They all have certain jobs to do, and these should cover the activities of the school necessary for the education of 500, 600, or whatever number of children. This is the acknowledged task of the school. But if this formal structure breaks down at any point, an informal structure, always present to some extent, takes over. For the probationers, this informal structure is often provided by other young teachers. This is, as we know from probationers' comments, often emotionally satisfying, but from the point of view of information and the task in hand, the result may be less than good.

One of the reasons for the probationers' satisfaction with the help which they commonly receive from their young colleagues derives from the fact that this relationship not only provides information, but also supplies their 'expressive' or emotional needs. These needs are difficult to meet in the formal structure of an organisation. It is difficult to determine by degree or by job allocation who shall be friendly with whom, who shall be hated, who can be leaned upon, who can be dominated, who can be cherished.

These needs are supplied more easily by the informal structure of the school. This is not to say that a formal organisation cannot determine and channel some emotional needs and feelings. It is illuminating to look round any staff room and notice how friendships or jealousies are determined by mutual responsibilities, or out-of-school activities, or relegation to teaching in the science block or the church hall.

A good Head should be able to meet both the 'task' needs, educating the children through the teachers, and some of the emotional 'expressive' needs of his staff, by acting as a repository for feelings of love, respect and hatred. But this is a complex role to fill, and it is also difficult for some young teachers to accept this rôle: the probationer finds it difficult to acknowledge that he can both like and dislike the Head, approve and disapprove, and do some jobs willingly and others with the greatest of reluctance. Hence in many schools, this knife-edged balance of feelings is made more easily bearable by splitting the rôle between the Head and his Deputy. The Head either does all the 'dirty work' and everybody loves the Deputy: 'A strict Head consistent with punishment and rewards. A firm but humanitarian Deputy-Head whom the boys respect but do not fear.' Or the Head is much beloved, but the Deputy-Head 'runs the school'. It may not be the best possible solution to a situation, but it can be acceptable and workable, if colleagues have not come to terms with ambivalent feelings in other ways. Splitting allows for displacement of unacceptable feelings on to another member of staff; the danger is that one member may become the recipient of all ill-feelings rightly belonging elsewhere: he may become the staff scapegoat. This is disastrous: better the scapegoating of the buildings, the L.E.A., the college, the department or the local adviser!

A newcomer to a school needs to listen to what is said

about its formal structure and then to look around and see where the informal structure lies and to whom affection, hostility, respect, etc., are directed. In this way, he will come to know, and it is hoped, accept his Head and colleagues and, in turn, be accepted by them.

4

Pupils and parents

Relationships with pupils

A quarter of the Leicester probationers said that the most enjoyable part of their first year's teaching was their relationships with children. This, to some, was quite unexpected: 'Surprising mutual affection between self and children.' 'Children' ranged in age from 7 to 18 or 19 years, and on the whole, one got the impression that the probationers who openly spoke of their affection were referring to younger children only. It is acceptable to acknowledge warm feelings towards younger pupils, but not usually towards older ones, towards adolescents. Feelings for older pupils may be strained by underlying sexual implications and the whole relationship may be further complicated by the rebellious attitude of many adolescents towards authority.

However, in addition to these emotional relationships with pupils, there were what might be described as intellectual partnerships, which also gave great satisfaction. The pleasure from noting 'unexpected insights shown by child' of 'seeing two of the children learning to read' of 'finding dull children will respond to *The Caucasian Chalk Circle*' and of 'being pestered with questions at the end of the lesson'. This different satisfaction is obviously related to the children acquiring information, seeing intellectual relationships, and picking up enthusiasm from the

57

teacher. It is a relationship based on the teacher's special skills and special knowledge.

Obviously, these two kinds of satisfactions open to teachers, making friends and finding workmates, cannot be completely separated from each other. The teacher feels an emotional warmth towards the pupil who does well. Nevertheless there is a difference which, it is clear from the comments of probationers, was appreciated by them. It could be explained—to use technical terms—by saying that pupils and teachers meet each other's expressive needs in the one case, by being mutually affectionate, and in the other case, they meet mutual task needs by helping in the job to be done. As was mentioned in Chapter 2, pupils expect teachers 'to teach' and new teachers get pleasure not only from being friendly with pupils, but finding that they can teach well.

And if they cannot, the opposite holds: 'I disliked most in my probationary year teaching a subject I was not fully in command of.' 'I hated the experience of constant repetition but the children remaining still muddled.' The absence of the necessary modicum of teaching skill and knowledge can, not only be immediately frustrating, but can undermine the probationer's confidence as well. That is, unless the probationer can find a scapegoat in the form of poor equipment, inadequate preparation in training, or unresponsive children. Former students often complain about being asked to teach other than their main subject, and an age group outside their expected range. Some teachers' courses allow for little manoeuvrability in the kind of job the new teacher is likely to do well, but some Heads and administrators cling too closely to the old elementary school idea of the all-purpose teacher. It makes filling posts apparently so much easier.

Whatever the age of the pupil, or whatever the subject taught, some teachers understand the introverted compliant child best and some can tolerate satisfactorily the aggressive boy or girl. Young teachers should not expect to get on equally well with all and should not be surprised if they find a few pupils particularly difficult. Some teachers like mothering children, some welcome helping the deprived, but some dislike, 'having to nurse as well as to teach'.

Nor should teachers be surprised if their pupils reactions to their approaches are not as reasonable as they feel they have a right to expect them to be. One young teacher taking part in a discussion group (Eldridge, 1964, 2, p. 59), complained that 'They are willing to talk about their subjects but they don't want to talk about yours. I did this. I talked about the Fair but they were not willing to discuss trees afterwards.' In the eyes of the pupil it is difficult to believe that 'Fairs' and 'trees' are equivalent and interchangeable. More and more it is being realised that we react not to the 'real' world but to the world as *we* see it, to a world created by our wishes, expectations and fears. Teachers may become aware of this in themselves: 'We interpreted being put in a tough school for teaching practice as a devious plan to fail us' (Nicholson, 1965, 4, p. 93), but are not always willing or perhaps able to accept the same devious thinking in their pupils. Indeed we tend to demand from others higher standards in reasonableness, good manners and moral principles than we do from ourselves. Teachers often expect their pupils to be more punctual, tidy, sincere, hard working, and altruistic than they have long ago given up expecting themselves to be.

Teachers should not be surprised if their actions are misinterpreted by pupils. Professor Blyth (1965, I, p. 107) makes this point in commenting on discipline in junior schools: 'When a punitive regime has flourished the introduction of a more permissive climate may readily be

59

mistaken for incompetence.' It requires very positive demonstration to the contrary by the new teacher—and a period of time—before the permissive climate is recognised for what it is. Assuming of course, that it is permissive by choice and not by default. A similar misunderstanding may occur when a new teacher is in the process of 'tightening up': his action may be seen by the children as entirely vindictive. Probationers—and other people beginning new jobs—have to be prepared to give time and effort to getting a new method of working and a new relationship accepted. The situation is helped along by the fact that people expect a certain degree of change with a new arrival, and indeed, may look forward to it, although loyalty to the predecessor may prevent them from acknowledging this. The probationer should not be discouraged by suspicious eyes and reluctant responses.

Obviously there are likely to be fewer misunderstandings, and an assured welcome, the more experiences the teacher and class have in common. This is *one* of the reasons why secondary modern schools present the greater problem for the new teacher. Few have been through these schools as pupils themselves, whereas most have spent some time in infant, junior and grammar schools.

Yet there are certain basic attitudes which influence a probationer's relationship with children whatever the type of school or wherever it happens to be. Compare the attitudes expressed, for example, in these comments: 'Don't go to be friendly to the children—they regard you as an enemy', with 'be firm but friendly, many boys are open and easily hurt'. So, of course, are many teachers. One defence against this is to expect the worst for then no disappointment can arise. Unfortunately expectations can be self-fulfilling and the worst becomes reality. The problem is to assess the situation—as far as one can—as it is, and to *work* skilfully for a happy and effective teaching

and learning relationship with the pupils. This will take
time and effort for many probationers.

Pupils in their teaching groups

No matter how the pupils are organised into groups within a school, whether into large classes, small family groups,
or sets, the teacher is the leader of the group. This is so
whatever the degree of freedom entailed, unless he has lost
his position as teacher, for he has given the freedom and
he can take it away again. The leadership implied in the
authoritarian organisation of a class is, of course, self
evident, that in a democratic set up may be masked.

Professor Waller in *The Sociology of Teaching* (1932)
draws attention to two kinds of leadership in schools (and
other institutions), institutionalised leadership and personal
leadership. Institutionalised leadership stems from a particular position in a society and is common to all members holding similar positions; personal leadership is unique
and develops from an individual's special abilities. The
leadership of the teacher always contains large elements
of the former, it depends on his status in the school society
and on his professional training. It can be helped and sup-
ported—or undermined—by various conditions present in
the school.

One of the conditions which helps to support institutionalised leadership is distancing. Distancing is made
easier by the custom, which we noticed in Chapter 2, of
giving the youngest forms in a school group to the probationer. On the face of it this seems to be a case of the
blind leading the blind, but in fact, the greater the age
difference, the greater the difference in years between
teacher and taught, the less the threat of the scholar to the
security of the new teacher and the more easily is he able
to hold his institutionalised leadership rôle. Probationers

differ in how much they like and depend on institutionalised leadership in teaching and how much they need
support to keep it effectively in being. The institutionalised
rôle is certainly important in the formal teaching situation
when the teacher stands in front of a class and deals with
it as a unit. Indeed the distancing important in such leadership is here seen clearly in spatial terms, the teacher is
physically at a distance from his class. This is not so when
the class is working in groups or doing individual assign-
ments and the teacher walks around. Some probationers
may find the loss of distancing disturbing but some may
wish to play down the institutionalised aspect of leadership in teaching anyway. It is a question of personality,
philosophy and training. The born raconteur, the teacher
who prefers the proscenium arch would wish to have the
whole form as an audience, while the student who finds
himself imperceptibly creeping to the front desks of the
class would probably be happier teaching small groups.
By the time he completes his training the new teacher
should have some idea which form of teaching he is best
able to do; how far he is dependent on institutionalised
leadership and how far he needs the help of extraneous
conditions to hold his leadership rôle.

Many probationers dislike teaching backward forms,
whether backward in the true meaning of the word or
merely backward in a relative sense, as, for example, the
lowest stream of a grammar school: 'I disliked working
for G.C.E. with the bottom streams.' But there are some
who enjoy 'the challenge of the lowest streams' which
frequently contain children with a large number of personal problems. It is in these forms that personal quirks and
individual steps in learning are most blatantly obvious. It
is here that there are certain elements of nursing, or helping the 'sick'. Some young teachers prefer to work under
these extreme conditions of inequality where children are

most obviously in need. Others dislike the nursing element
and the lack of scholarly work.

We have seen in Chapter 3 how the school and the forms
in it, have many elements of an extended family. In his
class a teacher acts, irrespective of his own desires, as a
mother or father figure, often a bit of both, to his pupils.
Whether the good or 'bad' elements in this situation will
be predominant will depend, at the beginning, on the previous experiences of the pupils, both at home and at
school. They will project their mother, father and teacher
figures on to the new teacher, who will in turn play the
mother, father and teacher rôles as previously experienced
by him. At first the success or failure of the probationer,
may well depend on situations largely out of his control.
Later his own personality and professional skills will come
into their own.

Obviously another factor determining how these rôles
will be played will be the age of the pupils. It is easy, for
most, but not all young teachers, to be a mother or father
to five or six year olds; considerably more difficult if the
pupils are ten years older.

In secondary schools, young teachers are often tempted
to play the 'peer group' rôle, leaving the mother and father
rôle to older members of the staff, and this may be a good
solution provided that the newcomer can retain the leadership of the group. There is, however, the ever present danger of being swept up completely into the 'peer group' of
pupils and losing one's identity as a teacher. In this case
the leadership of the class will depend solely on the personal leadership qualities of the probationer, he will have
given up the powers of leadership stemming from his
status as a teacher. The strain may be more than his personal qualities and professional skills can stand at this
point in his career.

This situation may have a further difficulty; the probationer's hostile feelings may be directed towards older members of the staff standing in father and mother rôles to him. A probationer who finds himself always siding with his pupils against older colleagues should take a long cool look at the situation in which he finds himself.

Co-educational schools

Peer group rôles for teachers are especially 'tricky' in co-educational secondary schools where sexual attractions are most likely to be felt between teacher and taught. Some young men are 'flattered by the attention of teen-age girls'; some are embarrassed by button-holing admirers and have to seek advice on how to discourage them without wounding their feelings. Obviously such crushes can have harmful consequences, not only to the two concerned, but to the form as a whole, as can the homosexual attractions which used to be common in single-sex schools.

Yet within these strongly felt relationships there are possibilities for good; the sexual element is often in a sublimated form and casts a glow over the teacher and what is being taught. If these relationships are recognised for what they are, and not encouraged, they will give a liveliness and inspiration to work in the classroom which it might otherwise lack. In any case these attractions occur between teacher and taught as in other walks of life. The probationer should be aware of them, and be able to recognise those which might cause trouble; he should realise the danger of a highly charged love turning to hate. Young teachers should be especially aware of using such situations as compensations for failures in their personal life and should make full use of professional status and etiquette in dealing with them.

Primary school teachers are spared this extra complication in school relationships although even they respond differently to small boys and small girls. They expect different things from them, as indeed do their parents. Sometimes this is openly acknowledged in a different curriculum and in in the form of different penalties for misbehaviour. For example, mixed schools frequently retain corporal punishment for boys, but do not use it with girls. Particularly is this the case with secondary schools. Such differences in treatment might be expected to generate resentment and indeed, this seems to be so. A Leicester man in a mixed comprehensive school said, 'Bad behaviour amongst lowest streams due to varying standards of punishable offence. No corporal punishment for girls, but corporal punishment for boys. Girls a bigger problem.' Another in a grammar school commented that the Head had difficulty with control, 'especially in dealing with difficult girls'. On the other hand, the following quotation speaks of a very different experience : 'The school was one of all boys, tough boys generally and punishments have always been severe—caning and slippering. I left this school after one year and at my new school (mixed) I have never used a cane and the Head is against caning except as a last resort.' Other probationers have commented on the 'civilising' effect of girls.

In fact in spite of the sprinkling of problems about discipline peculiar to co-educational schools, there is no evidence that discipline as a whole is better, or worse, than it is in single-sex schools. Yet it seems likely that sex differences within a school add an extra dimension, for good or ill, to the learning and discipline situation within it.

Co-educational schools show up most clearly any difficulties or adjustments, associated with the earlier physical maturity of children compared with, say, ten years ago. In junior schools, in top classes, sex has begun to be seen in almost adolescent terms, while in secondary schools one might say that there has been a similar developmental upgrading, so that what was merely adolescent has become near-adult. These changes will obviously be influencing single-sex schools too. In order to deal with the earlier maturity, it is more than ever necessary that the new teacher should not feel less than adult.

The academic attainment of pupils

As we have seen, probationers get a good deal of pleasure out of actually teaching a subject well, feeling that their pupils now know much more than they did. As a corollary to this they feel frustrated if the children do not learn. Twelve per cent of the Aberdeen probationers gave unresponsive pupils as one of their major sources of dissatisfaction. These pupils are usually— but not always—thought of as backward.

New teachers are often unaware of how relative a term this is. Consider for example, the following comments from Leicester probationers in different areas: 'The top form each year is good, the middle average, while the other is, I feel, well below grammar school ability,' and 'About one third would be more suited to a Sec. Mod.', together with 'the third stream are definitely not grammar school types at all'. Obviously all these probationers were wanting to lose the bottom third of their schools, irrespective of the cultural standard of their town and number of grammar schools in it. This suggests that some at least of the backwardness of these pupils resides not in themselves, but in being in the bottom third of the school!

A few young teachers are aware of the part played by teachers' attitudes and the school hierarchy in the creation of such fringe forms: 'A large express stream (about 50) disheartens many others' and, 'Generally the sixth form standard was high but there were a number of "slum" forms lower down in the school—products of a streaming system now abandoned.' But streaming need not have this effect. One young teacher said, 'Top stream borderline grammar, lower stream looked after too.' Obviously much depends on the school in which the beginner finds himself. It is difficult, though not impossible, to stand out against the unstated assumption and self-fulfilling prophecies of the organisation in which one is working. Young teachers need to watch their own reactions to pupils who are at the bottom of the school hierarchy, and whose teachers have their noticeable successes elsewhere, and decide how far the poor attainment of the pupils is due, at least in part, to the attitude and organisation of the school.

Probationers naturally tend to think if they return to a school similar to the one they attended as a child that they can make certain assumptions about the work and the pupils in it. But with the present rate of educational change this is not so. A few probationers mentioned, for example, what might be described as a new kind of backwardness, the low ability of some sixth form pupils in terms of 'A' level work. One probationer's special problem was 'Finding useful linguistic activities for a backward VI A,' and another's, 'teaching "A" level French form to a VI form, 88% of whom had failed "O" level'. This 'high-level backwardness' was something for which the probationers felt they had been ill prepared but which is likely to become common with the increase in size of sixth forms and its change of structure.

Occasionally, of course, bright children present a problem too. But it is very much a minority problem, as seen by young teachers; two per cent of the Birmingham probationers mentioned difficulties with bright children and occasionally a Leicester teacher gave as a special difficulty such situations as 'A very lively and intelligent VI form,' or

'Difficulty in achieving friendly contact with form IV A, the star form of the school'. Many more thoroughly enjoyed their bright forms, whether they were bright according to any standard, or bright for that particular school.

When asked if they had any comments to make about the academic standards of the pupils in their schools, the Leicester teachers most frequently talked in terms of home-background, although some mentioned the influence of school organisation—as we have already seen—and a few also wrote about the stimulating effect of good examination results. Home background was seen almost entirely in terms of its harmful effects. Probationers who mentioned its positive assets, like the probationer in a hard working Yorkshire mill town, were rare. There were common complaints that 'The population of the city is below average in intelligence,' or 'the area seems to be poor in innate ability, anyway, predominantly working class'. But blame was not limited to the working classes. There was also middle-class apathy: 'Mostly children of small tradesmen with prosperous but uncultured home background.'

Only occasionally did a probationer suggest that the achievement of the pupils might be related to the standard of the teaching of the staff: 'Gifted, enlightened teachers', 'Academic standards of staff not impressive'; or to the kind of work which they were asked to do; 'G.C.E.-type syllabuses unsatisfactory' and 'improved facilities for non-selective pupils'. The new teachers found it difficult to write about the attainment of pupils in terms of the teachers' level of skill.

Obviously some teachers will be more skilful with some pupils rather than others. Some like to teach 'selective' and 'non-selective' children together; others disapprove or find this too demanding. Some enjoy a school where there is a 'very good G.C.E. record, impressive list of old boys'. Others would feel themselves put in the shade by the

68

achievement of these pupils or object to the old school tie approach. Some probationers like children who come from 'country districts' who are 'placid by nature'; others find these children dull.

Discipline in schools

'I have realised that good discipline makes for good academic work.' This seems simple and straightforward enough as stated by a Leicester probationer but in fact the whole question of discipline is complex and anything but straightforward. What is clear is that the concept of 'discipline' looms large in the minds of young teachers, particularly those in secondary schools. Dr. Edmonds in *The First Year of Teaching* (1966, p. 11), states that extension of probation is due most frequently to 'poor class management . . .' and 'basic inability to secure discipline . . . particularly at secondary school level'. So probationers are right to be concerned. Poor discipline is also one of the few things in teaching which is inevitably a public affair; all the class knows and finally the whole school cannot help but know.

Good discipline can, of course, be private and inward : one talks of a well-disciplined mind and stable personality, but actually when students and young teachers speak of discipline they are usually thinking primarily of indiscipline, of noise and chaos which require the application of certain external disciplinary measures. They expect discipline to be enforced and are surprised when it is just *there* : 'It is constantly a topic of conversation in the staff room as to why discipline is good because rules are few and punishment fairly rare.'

However in spite of the stress on the externally imposed discipline, many probationers are well aware of the importance of attitudes and assumptions expressed in the

69

school generally in accounting for the good and largely non-assertive discipline, which they find: 'A very happy atmosphere in the school—cordial relations between staff and girls. Very young staff. Attractive Headmistress with a modern outlook.' And—'The senior master rapidly earned a reputation for firmness and fairness and a workmanlike atmosphere soon prevailed'. Poor discipline is also seen as a general school problem, a general malaise, but this occurs less frequently. One of these rarer instances was: 'Poor leadership from the Head and generally speaking weak staff who did not really care. Ability of the children to cope was very limited and this, allied to a certain roughness in the background, meant they had little respect for the school.'

These explanations are all school-centred and there were many more of a similar kind, together with rather different ones, such as 'a strict Head', 'a core of respected older members of staff', 'splendid games and recreation facilities, they let off steam in their own time', 'not too many rules', 'good prefect system with delegation of authority', and, as the other side of the coin, 'the school operated in three buildings', 'ten centres of authority in the form of housemasters', 'Headmaster unreasonably strict disciplinarian', and of a rather different kind, 'novels and poetry anthologies too difficult and adult, the children rebelled through sheer boredom'.

Other explanations of good or bad discipline are given in terms of the homes of the children and these frequently stress the importance of stable home background. On the whole the homes tend to be called in more frequently to account for good school discipline rather than bad: 'pupils have church background', 'rural children much more docile than town children'.

The probationers often notice subtle differences between home backgrounds. One remarked on the advantage of not having large cohesive outside groups of adolescents, from the same housing estate, coming into a school. Another understood the disturbing influence of living in a changing home community: 'the exceptions [to good behaviour] were two troublesome groups from changing rural fringes'.

These two comments and others, show that probationers are aware of the part played by home background in bad behaviour, but the tendency (at least among Leicester probationers) was to mention more frequently the contribution a good home had to good behaviour in schools. This was interesting in the light of the opposite tendency when talking about the children's academic achievement. In the latter case it was only rarely suggested that the home made any helpful contribution, although home background was freely sighted in the case of academic failure. It looks as if the young teacher sees himself as essentially active as an agent of change. If no change takes place, if the children are dull and no knowledge is imparted or if the children are good and no discipline actively exerted, then he sees himself and his colleagues as not teaching, the situation having been taken over by outside influences.

So far all the impressions on discipline have been given from the probationers' point of view. Most seem likely to be reasonably correct, but some will not be so. An unexpected characteristic of probationers who fail their probationary year, is an 'inability to accept advice' (Edmonds, 1966, p. 11). This usually goes along with an inability to see that it is needed; as one Head said 'I find it hard to convince him that, from my observations, his junior forms are not working owing to his lack of observation of what they are doing'. Some probationers are, at first, curiously insensitive to what is actually going on in the classroom.

But there is one aspect of discipline in many schools

71

which cannot fail to be observed, and that is corporal punishment. The implications and repercussions may well be missed. The attitude of Leicester probationers to corporal punishment, like that of Headmasters, ranged from those who believed it necessary for good discipline, 'the right to beat', to those who denied its efficiency, 'the Headmaster was far too brutal with the children', and those who were prepared to accept it, in a particular school, 'older members of staff were strict disciplinarians of the pre-war variety, i.e. favoured iron hand and the cane— essential in this type of school', which was a modern school.

In fact from the comments of these probationers, it appears that there is generally speaking, a difference of attitude to discipline and corporal punishment between grammar and other schools, although a few schools in all types have corporal punishment. To take one small point first, the probationers were asked what they enjoyed most in their first year : four said 'good control'. These few were all teaching in modern schools. The probationers in these schools, and in junior and comprehensive, mentioned Heads and colleagues relatively more frequently than children, when talking about discipline. 20% of modern school probationers listed corporal punishment among the factors influencing school discipline, whereas only 2% of grammar school probationers did so.

Discipline would appear to be more frequently imposed and to be more openly aggressive in modern schools. Certainly these schools contain a higher percentage of working-class pupils, from a social background in which physical aggression is accepted and these schools would, therefore, find it more difficult to use other forms of school discipline even if they wanted to—and some obviously did not want. But as we have said, by no means all probationers in schools using corporal punishment agreed with it: 'use of corporal punishment widespread and this in my opinion does not make for good discipline'. One probationer, at least, had seen it fail. He suggested that training should be given during the education year on how to use it successfully!

This suggestion will probably bring a recoil of horror from most people. There is a tendency to exclude during the training course any discussion of discipline in these terms. We deal with discipline as it arises from school organisations, keeping people busy, careful lesson preparation and so on, but we find it almost impossible to talk about corporal punishment as a means of imposing authority. This leaves the former student ill-prepared to consider the school situation objectively and, if necessary, put forward convincingly other points of view. It is a question of helping the probationers to reconcile Bryan Wilson's comment (1962, p. 25) 'Affection is the first language which man understands and it becomes the lever by which all other languages can be initially learned,' with the small girl's statement to her teacher 'you're allowed to hit us, but not to call us names, my Mother said so' (Eldridge, 1964, 2, p. 58).

Non-corporal punishments may have an unpleasant side too. One probationer analysed the situation in her school thus:

> 'discipline was based largely on fear and the fact that so many people heard about trouble and dealt with it. Children tended to like or respect, seldom both. Exposure of worst offenders to entire school (2,000 odd) in prayers. Real delinquents, however, got away with almost everything—staff afraid of them. Negative action often taken, e.g. keep known ill-behaved children out of concerts—treats—before they get a chance to behave well or badly.'

Obviously this probationer disapproved of the situation

73

but the methods of discipline she described are fairly
common in schools and many teachers would approve of
them. Other probationers, luckier or wiser in their choice
of schools, welcomed 'positive encouragement rather than
threats', appreciated the habit of 'treating children as responsible and mature' and enjoyed a 'generally happy
atmosphere and easy relations between staff and boys'.

Possibly relaxed pleasant schools attract relaxed pleasant
probationers and strict formal schools, strict formal probationers. Moeller and Charters (1965) in the United States
found that different types of school systems appeared to
employ different types of teachers—or very rapidly caused
them to change towards their particular type of system.
Possibly something similar happens here.

It would be a mistake to think that *most* new teachers
are disturbed by discipline problems and that of those who
are, it is anything more than a passing phase. It is interesting to notice that whereas 30% of the Leicester secondary
school probationers gave discipline as their special problem, a smaller proportion described their schools as having
'rather poor' discipline generally. (25% in modern and
comprehensive schools and 17% in grammar). The probationers, as a whole, described their discipline in the first
year as worse than that of their schools.

Battling with disorganised classes can be a strain and
this showed in the health record of the Leicester probationers. A significantly higher proportion working in
junior, comprehensive and modern schools with rather
poor discipline had absences from school.

Some probationers tried to improve their class control
by careful preparation of lessons, the introduction of more
practical work, simplifying lessons for less able pupils and
'tightening up'. A few found it a help to get to know their
pupils in outside activities. Many had advice and backing
from the staff and Head. The modern school probationers

74

received, apparently the least help from their colleagues, while the comprehensive school probationers had most—and still wanted more.

The advice which the young teachers said they would give to newcomers to their schools often centred around discipline. In general they made four main points. The first was, briefly, to be knowledgeable: 'Learn the school routine, coming in and going out, meals procedures, etc., 'discover school disciplinary system early in career—children always expect young teachers not to be aware of, or use, this'. The second point had two key phrases: one was 'right from the beginning' and the other 'be strict and firm'. This warning derives from what the probationers thought of as their own laxness but which their Heads often saw as 'a need to be liked'. The third point, which related to the second, was the importance of making the correct first impression. The directions given here varied, however, with the school and personality of the probationer and ranged from 'Try to show the children you are human, have a sense of humour', to 'Be a swine for the first four weeks'. The fourth and last point was a plea for the acceptance of the less than perfect, a warning not to expect too much: 'Be prepared to have plans upset, lose lesson time for staff meetings, extra-long assemblies, and have lessons interrupted by people doing errands.' And 'In the type of school in which I am teaching disciplinary problems are bound to take precedence in the first year of experience'. At the end of that time most probationers will be able to join with the probationer who said 'I feel much more confident now'.

Parents

This section on the relationship of probationers to the parents of their pupils comes last in this chapter, and these relationships, except indirectly, come last in the minds of most probationers. We have seen that they are well aware of the importance of the home but one hears very little about actually meeting or talking to parents. In Chapter 2 we noted that primary school teachers were the ones who were most occupied with P.T.A. meetings and parents' days: other teachers much less so. This difference was based, of course, on a small number of graduate primary probationers, but the evidence from the Aberdeen and Birmingham enquiry supports the impression that parents were more actively concerned with primary schools. This is probably because the teaching in them can be more easily thought of as an extension of home 'teaching' and because the age of the child makes the parents feel, and claim, more responsibility for him. This can create problems. It was in terms of these that primaray school probationers in Aberdeen and Birmingham mentioned parents. In Aberdeen it was the primary school probationers who were most dissatisfied with their relationships with parents and in Birmingham it was also the primary school probationers who were most frequently given guidance on this relationship. It seems hedged around with uncertainties and one Leicester junior school probationer said, 'Attack the parents first, before they attack you'. On the other hand who has not heard of junior schools with swimming baths, orchestral instruments and cameras all supplied by parents!

Inevitably there must often be under the very real mutual interest and co-operation, latent antagonism between school and parents, especially at the primary school level, a certain jealousy of the influence exerted over children when in the other's care, a certain tendency to blame each other when things go wrong, a partial knowledge of conditions in the home or the school which makes false conclusions easy.

Young teachers are not always sufficiently aware of these conflicts, or forget them under the pressure of a new job. The teacher's very newness, his recent crossing of the dividing line between family loyalty and school loyalty may make him all the more wary of the family pull. Relationships between parents and probationers may well need guidance. One student, at least, recognised the necessity of educating the parents as well as the children, of getting their co-operation in dealing with the children's school problems. He suggested that some sort of health visitor should be employed to make contact with the parents. In some countries this would be expected of the teacher himself.

On the other hand, many students already enjoy 'Good Parent/Staff relationships via P.T.A.' The Birmingham probationers who reported being given a good deal of advice about parents reported no special problems concerning them. Understanding the parents makes a mutual understanding and sympathy between teacher and pupils much more likely.

5

Plans for the probationary year

The problem

The previous four chapters provide a picture of lively differences among probationers in schools; differences of experience and attitude. Certain outstanding features are worth considering from the point of view of helping probationers—and schools—to avoid failure and develop promise, during the first year.

Schools are much more alike than they used to be but there are still marked differences between infant, junior, grammar, modern and comprehensive schools; not only in the kind of teaching (which one would expect) but also in attitudes of the Head to his staff and the staff to their pupils, expectations about non-teaching school activities, and even towards money; the Birmingham men in modern schools complained twice as frequently about salaries as did those in junior schools! There are also differences associated with the size of the schools; in 9,000 primary schools a probationer will have one full time colleague only (Blyth, 1965, p. 165), whereas in some large schools he may find himself one of twenty probationers on the same staff (Edmonds, 1966, p. 4). Geographical areas carry school differences along with them; slow fen children and sharp Cockneys. Within a town there are high class suburbs and underprivileged areas. It seems an overwhelming task to prepare students for such diversity.

To set against this variety, however, there are certain limits suggested by the nature of students' first posts. Many probationers like to go home to teach and a smaller, but sizeable proportion, take posts near to their colleges or departments. Probationers, and particularly women probationers, are given the youngest group in the school to teach. Advantages should be taken of these customs.

Probationers vary tremendously in the time which they spend on their professional work. Schools, modern schools in particular, in their turn, vary in the information which they give to probationers before the session begins. Nevertheless there are certain common problems which tend to harass young teachers; poor discipline in secondary schools, poor class management in primary schools, backward children of all ages and difficult relationships with older colleagues. All these take their toll, together with the very newness of the situation in which the probationer finds himself. Those probationers in the more 'protected' teaching situations, those for example, who have trained and teach in familiar schools, in grammar schools, usually have fewer absences from school.

The problem is to discover what the 'partners involved' to quote the N.U.T. and A.T.C.D.E. (1961, p. 2), can do to minimise the difficulties and make probation more positive; 'the last phase of initial training', helpful to both the good and the poor new teacher. Several useful suggestions have already been put forward by Kitson, Sealey and others (1966), and by Edmonds (1966) in *The First Year of Teaching*. To these is added the approach described here; one centred essentially on more circumscribed preparation and more indirect supervision.

Tutors in colleges and departments of education

Obviously tutors in colleges and departments of education

believe that they already try to help their students as much as possible to prepare themselves for their first posts. It would be worthwhile finding out, however, if the preparation might not be more effective if it were more definitely geared to the most common types of post taken by their students. For the actual forms within schools, this would be for women, the first forms, and for men the slightly older classes. Stress on preparation for these forms has already been implemented in Finland (Koskenniemi, 1965) and in one or two colleges here.

The schools themselves in which probationers get their first posts are frequently in the home area of the probationers. It would seem very reasonable therefore, to have one of the teaching practices in those areas. The students would then know something of the schools from a teacher's point of view and the L.E.A. would know something of its possible future employees. These experiences would provide a wealth of material (students usually come from scattered areas of England and Wales) for courses in educational theory and method and the students would get the opportunity, under guidance, of relating college work with school situations.

Tutors often complain that their former students rapidly forget what they have been taught in college or department and conform to school opinions. This should occasion no surprise when one remembers how powerful group opinion is; witness the experiments of Asch (1952) in making people misjudge the length of lines. However, it has also been shown that individuals are best able to stand up to the onslaught of another point of view if they have been 'innoculated' against it by having its arguments presented to them in small 'doses' first (Hovland *et al*, 1966). A session in school followed by discussions about methods experienced there, but differing from those advocated by tutors, could help to stabilise opinions about methods and attitudes—not necessarily of course in the direction wished by the tutor.

The difficulty of giving some supervision to the teaching practice of students scattered to home towns in this way could be overcome by enrolling the help of teachers in looking after them. Such an arrangement would be excellent for several reasons. First there are many good teachers whose art is too confined to a school or a class. There are others whose work has wilted through lack of stimulus from outside recognition; this could easily be revived. Secondly, teachers and schools thus concerned with the training of students would be more likely to offer suitable assistance to probationers. They would know more, would understand probationers' points of view and to some extent would identify themselves with their progress. Thirdly tutors and teachers would be more closely linked professionally and this would help to get rid of the antagonism which sometimes exists between departments, colleges and schools. It would also enhance the status of the teaching profession.

This school-centred teaching practice would, of course, involve a reconsideration of the kind of help and supervision given to students during teaching practice. To a large extent the teacher would have to act as the student's tutor during this period. Institutions would have to choose the arrangements for teacher responsibility which most suited both of them; several types of teacher-tutor schemes are described by John Baker (1967) but others could be evolved. Such an arrangement with schools would have important side advantages. It would, for example, introduce much closer liaison with local education authorities, for their officers would be called upon to suggest suitable schools to colleges and departments. This administrative association would then make it easier for an exchange of views concerning the probationary year of former students.

L.E.A. officials

The importance of L.E.A. officials in making probation more worthwhile cannot be overestimated. They can set the pattern for the educational activities which go on in their area. They stand outside the schools and can act as an authority and a centre of advice to which probationers can appeal if necessary; they can act as an essential third party. It would be a helpful distinction between teaching practice and probation if L.E.A. officers could remain outside the former but be more actively concerned in the latter.

One important part which they could play should start well before the probationer sets foot in a school. I mean by this that the L.E.A. offering the post, or permitting a Head to do so, should know exactly what kind of job is being offered to the new recruit. What class, or classes will be taught, what subjects needed. What participation in out-of-school activities is expected. How much of this information will be passed on to the probationer before school begins. Some schools need an adviser's help before the probationer ever goes near them. A Head who has had frequent changes of staff, or who has been for sometime without a full complement, or who has had to modify his school policy and teaching techniques may well need assistance in preparing for a newcomer. In any case in all schools the adviser needs to check with the Head the apparent abilities of the student against the demands of the post which he is about to fill, and to give help when necessary in remedying any omission of information or skills.

The living arrangements of the probationer in the new

community are of almost equal importance with the teaching arrangements within the school. L.E.A.'s can help here by making sure, as a matter of routine, that appropriate clubs, churches, societies in the community know of the arrival of probationers. In some areas it should be possible, particularly on new housing estates, to provide 'club' houses, where, say ministers, nurses, social workers, as well as teachers could live. These would require daily domestic help, because however well young teachers believe they can look after themselves, they do in fact, benefit from being 'mothered' during the first year out.

A proportion of L.E.A.'s have, for some time, been holding at least one meeting each session for probationers to introduce them to each other and to the local advisers and the educational facilities provided by the authority. This habit needs further development. One Chief Inspector of Schools has recently published a report on a successful experiment (Dalrymple, 1967), consisting of a series of discussions and lectures with probationers and Heads, during the probationary year. Meetings for probationers at the end of the session and at the beginning of the second year, while useful in themselves, cannot be considered a way of helping probationers; the best or the worst will have happened by then.

The function of the L.E.A. officials is, as I see it, to make the school and local environments educationally stimulating and personally rewarding to the new probationer. They are the essential back-room boys.

School staff

The key member of the school in dealing with probationers is, as in so many things, the Head, irrespective of whether he makes himself personally responsible for looking after them or whether he hands this task over to his staff. There is a good case for more frequently doing the latter, thus incorporating in the formal structure of the school what frequently goes on informally. Such an arrangement might help to take care of the problem of one person both guiding and assessing a probationer by virtually dividing these rôles between the Head and a senior teacher. Also, in these days of rapid staff turnover, the Head may find his time occupied not only with helping probations to fit into the school but with helping a depleted and insecure staff to adjust itself to probationers. A Head should not hesitate to ask for help from L.E.A. advisers, institutes, departments and colleges of education if his school is going through a difficult patch, which happens in most schools from time to time.

There are, to my mind, three main ways in which a Head can help a probationer either directly, or through the delegation of his powers. The first is by the selection of appropriate responsibilities for him, the second is through encouraging the educational interests of his staff and the third is by undertaking unobtrusive methods of training.

The responsibilities of many secondary school probationers could be made more manageable by giving them parallel forms to teach. This would cut down the excessive hours of preparation undertaken by some and make it easier to insist on an increase by others. It would also give probationers the opportunity of practising a lesson several times in succession and provide a breathing space in which to look over the results of teaching pupils of different levels of ability. Primary schools do not provide these opportunities of limiting responsibilities in the same way. Other methods have to be used. L.E.A.'s could assist by using peripatetic teachers, whose sole purpose would be to go round to the more difficult primary schools, freeing probationary teachers, at certain times in the week.

Encouraging the educational interests of his older staff may appear to be a devious way of helping young teachers but, in my opinion, the lack of up-to-date educational knowledge and experience among the staff of many schools is a major cause of the difficulties encountered in absorbing probationers profitably and happily into them. The ignorance of the older staff often creeps on them unawares and arises from the schools' relative intellectual and social isolation. It means however, that information and experiences of the latest educational ideas and techniques are limited to the newest and youngest recruit on the staff. Older members are immediately put at a disadvantage and this makes the defence of entrenched opinions inevitable and likely to be conducted with vigour—and some success. The Plowden Report, *Children in their Primary Schools* (1967), suggests that inservice training should be available for teachers every five years. This should provide more teachers with up-to-date information of their own and help them to play an active part in the training of probationers.

How unobtrusive is it possible to make this training? Is the Head going to drop into lessons? Should a senior teacher take over the class and give a demonstration lesson? Are schemes of work to be presented every Monday morning? Should a 'free' period be set aside for a tutorial every week? How unobtrusive in fact can effective assistance be made to be?

It would, I believe, be profitable to consider the whole question afresh, to develop an approach quite different from the guidance to which most probationers have been accustomed during their student days, thus helping them to progress from students to teachers. The kind of supervision given to social case workers (Young, 1967) would be eminently worth considering for probationers in schools. It would be a new experience for virtually all concerned. It obviates the necessity for the Head, or other teacher to

85

visit a probationer's class, but it demands a careful review of a series of lessons.

In the training of social workers no supervisor ever sits in and watches the workers deal with their clients. If the supervisor were there too, this would alter profoundly the relationship between the worker and his client. Hence all the training is accomplished by the supervisor discussing with the worker his case reports and taking up with him any points raised. The supervisor begins from where the case worker is, where *he* sees his problems to lie, moving out to further considerations later, thus helping the case worker to learn and acquire skill in his profession. Young teachers could be trained in the same way.

Some Heads who believe in giving unobtrusive assistance to probationers, and hesitate to undermine their prestige by openly helping them in school, already use what might be called a version of this technique. They concentrate on lesson discussion and a review of the pupils' work done in lessons. To move over to the full social case worker approach would only require a slanting towards more reporting on lessons and rather less on preparation, to-gether with practice and advice to Heads in understanding more clearly what is implied in reports as well as what is actually written or said.

Caspari and Eggleston (1965) have conducted an experi-ment on these lines with mature Diploma students who helped young college students on their teaching practice without, in fact, seeing them teach. This method is, I be-lieve, particularly suited to the final stages in training and therefore well worth investigating in relation to proba-tioners.

Probationers

Probation is usually spoken of in terms which imply that everyone beginning to teach in a school has just completed a course of training and is about to take up a teaching post for the first time. This, of course, is not true. Statistics quoted in *Teachers and Their First Posts* (N.U.T. and A.T.C.D.E., 1961) showed that over a quarter of the permanent appointments in 1958-1959 were given to untrained graduates and to specialists. The situation may be somewhat different now, but is certainly not entirely changed. In addition many temporary appointments of teachers are made: no less than one third of the Birmingham men and one sixth of the women in junior schools must have had such appointments for they had taught for more than nine months before going to college. As probationers they already had at least one year of teaching behind them. What effect these groups of mixed experience have on probationers generally is not known, but obviously the experienced probationers themselves must feel differently. Presumably they require less help.

There are, on the other hand, new teachers which generally speaking require more: we know, for example, that untrained graduates in maintained schools tend to be generally less successful and less committed (Collins, 1964). In some schools these untrained graduates and new temporary teachers must limit the assistance which can be given to what might be called bona fide probationers. Untrained graduates come, of course, under section 'B' of the 'rules' for probation and are under the surveillance of H.M.I.'s but their presence in, for example, junior schools, must often make extra demands on the staff.

Frequently probationers, trained and untrained, are worried about the probationary year. The N.U.S. and N.U.T. have recently issued a leaflet, *Teachers and Probation*, in an attempt to alleviate unnecessary fears. This is very helpful, but probationers are bound to have times of stress; the first year in any new job inevitably has moments of anxiety.

Former students often find a school restrictive after the freedom of college and university. To people who have had other jobs it may seem relatively free. This was certainly so with a Leicester chemist who had previously worked in industry; he prized the freedom of his first teaching post. One of the difficulties is that school restrictions easily overflow into restrictions out of school. Professor Blyth (1965, p. 20) comments that, 'Schools are a repository of ideals, and teachers by their lives, manners, morals and dress are expected to express them.' Not all teachers, particularly young teachers find this easy to do. If a probationer finds it difficult to conform to the general expectations about schools and teachers then he would be wise to choose his school and residence with care. In any case a probationer, when choosing a post should consider what he expects to get out of it and what he, himself, intends to give. Rather more, we hope than the girl who was, to quote her Headmistress, 'Appointed to this school 1.11.62 and left in July 1963, during which time she had eleven weeks maternity leave and prior to that, sixteen days absence in five separate weeks'. If a probationer has chosen a job because it is near home and has put its educational suitability second, then he must plan his work accordingly. Compensations elsewhere, in the form of a happy contented home and non-professional interest, may help him eventually to be very effective in his post.

This question of the educational suitability of a post requires to be taken more seriously than it is wont to be because of the variety of work developing in schools at the moment: the 'new mathematics', i.t.a., team teaching, programmed learning, the integregated day, the teacher-social worker approach and so on. All these demand special professional knowledge and are more acceptable to some personalities than others. The prospective applicant for a particular post should ask himself whether he has the necessary professional skills, and, if not, how he can acquire them.

'Combined operations'

It is not, as yet, at all clear what probationers can reasonably be expected to do when they begin teaching and what kinds of skills can be left to be developed during the probationary year. A consensus of opinion on this question is urgently required and would make for more realistic expectations on the part of everybody concerned. It would help to clarify the part to be played by colleges and departments of education, L.E.A.'s and schools to set more limited goals for the young teacher at each stage in his career. At the moment there are certain contradictions: the probationer should certainly be able to keep registers, but he need not necessarily be able to look after a form; he cannot be responsible for a department but he will have been trained to work in with someone who can; he may need help in looking after relationships with children but it can be assumed that he can get on with his colleagues in the staff room. There has been virtually no attempt to sort out conflicting expectations such as these, nor to give help in any systematic way to Heads and senior colleagues in the management of the first year's teaching of probationers.

Two years ago (1966), H.M.S.O. published a small booklet called *Supervisory Training. A New Approach for Management* by Meade and Greig. While not intended, of course, for schools it is interesting to consider in the context of teaching. It begins by pointing out that the training of supervisors has a history in three stages: first, 'Supervisors are born not made'; second, 'the common skills approach'; third, 'the training of supervisors on the job'. If one substitutes 'teachers' for supervisors the methods have a familiar ring. Probation as an extension of training, is training on the job, with the Head as a stand-in for the manager and the pupils for workers. It is worth-while, therefore, to see what is recommended. Meade and Greig's approach stresses the importance of training the trainers, i.e. the managers, or in our terms, the Heads and senior teachers of schools. Without this training, managers or Heads are thought of as being 'born and not made'; this is little different from thinking of supervisors, or teachers, in these terms.

Meade and Greig also advocate a careful analysis of the job to be done, the kind of activities involved. The train-ing of probationers in these terms is rare. There is little analysis of the job of teaching and Heads are not given guidance on how best to continue the training of the new teachers. This is where the L.E.A. officials should come in. Their rôle, as I see it, in the refashioning of the probation-ary year, is not only to give direct help in schools but also to provide for the training of the trainers, by laying on the necessary experimental courses for Heads and senior colleagues.

Probation, prepared for more precisely before its onset, and supervised indirectly by more educationally involved schools, should increase the art and skill of teachers, and raise the status of the teaching profession. More could then join with this Leicester probationer in saying 'A very good school, it will be difficult to leave'.

Suggestions for further reading

Chapter 1

BLYTH, W. A. L., *English Primary Education*, Vol. 1. Schools (Routledge & Kegan Paul, 1965). Chapter 7. This discusses the expectations about adults employed in primary schools.

EDMONDS, E. L., 'Problems of School Inspection', *Researches and Studies*, No. 22. December, 1961, pp. 28-43 (University of Leeds Institute of Education). An interesting historical account of the origins and functions of school inspectors in relation to the social milieu of their times.

N.U.T. and A.T.C.D.E. *Teachers in their first posts*, 1961. A most important booklet stressing the importance of the probationary year, and containing joint recommendations from the N.U.T. and A.T.C.D.E.

Chapter 2

The Young Teacher (Department of Education, Kings College, Newcastle-on-Tyne, 1955). Contains a useful historical survey and a chapter on the respective responsibilities of the college, L.E.A. and the school towards the probationary teacher.

EDMONDS, E. L., *The First Year of Teaching* (N.U.T., 1967). A booklet giving a clear exposition of the procedures involved in probation and the type of help available in

cases of difficulty. It also contains suggestions for the
future.

PLOWDEN REPORT, Central Advisory Council of Education
(England), *Children in their Primary Schools*, Vol. 1,
1967, Chapter 5, for the discussion on the 'Educational
Priority Areas'.

Chapter 3

PHILLIPS, M., *Small Social Groups in England* (Methuen,
1965). Chapter 13. Records of relationships between the
teaching staff within several schools.

NICHOLSON, C., 'A Kind of Guidance', *The New Era*, March,
April and May, 1965. Recordings of discussions with
young teachers.

RICHARDSON, E., *Group Study for Teachers* (Routledge and
Kegan Paul, 1967). Chapter 4. Explores the implication
of the position of furnitures, rooms, etc.

Chapter 4

ELDRIDGE, G., 'Gossamers & Anchors', *The New Era*, Nos.
1, 2 and 3, 1964. Recording of discussions between the
Head, Deputy Head and probationers in a girls' secondary modern school, many of which were much concerned with problems of pupils' behaviour.

WILSON, B. R., The Teacher's Rôle, *British Journal of
Sociology*, 1962, pp. 15-32. Teaching in present-day
society.

Chapter 5

DALRYMPLE, A. H., 'The Inservice Training of Probationary
Teachers', *Education for Teaching*. Summer 1967, pp. 48-
52. An example of 'combined operations'. L.E.A. officials,

Heads of schools and probationers took part in this experimental approach.

KOSKENNIEMI, M., *The Development of Young Elementary School Teachers* (University of Helsinki, 1965). An interesting account of what happens in Finland.

Bibliography

ASCH, S. E. (1952) *Social Psychology*, New York: Prentice Hall.

BAKER, J. R. (1967) 'A Teacher Co-Tutor Scheme', *Education for Teaching*, No. 73, pp. 25-30.

BLYTH, W. A. L. (1965) *English Primary Education*, London: Routledge & Kegan Paul. Vols. 1 and 2.

CASPARI, I. E. and EGGLESTON, S. J. (1965) 'A New Approach to Supervision of Teaching Practice', *Education for Teaching*, No. 68, pp. 42-52.

CENTRAL ADVISORY COUNCIL OF EDUCATION (ENGLAND) (1967) *Children in their Primary Schools*, London: H.M.S.O., Vol. I.

CHAZAN, M. (1963) 'The First Year of Teaching', *Times Educational Supplement*, 1.2.1963.

CLARK, R. P. and NISBET, J. D. (1963) *The First Two Years of Teaching*, Report published privately, Aberdeen University and College of Education.

COLLINS, M. (1959) 'Follow-up Study of some Former Graduate Student Teachers', *British Journal of Educational Psychology*, XXIX, pp. 187-197.

COLLINS, M. (1960) 'Health, Family and Teaching', *Universities Quarterly*, XIV, pp. 57-66.

COLLINS, M. (1964) 'Untrained and Trained Graduate Teachers. A comparison of their experiences during the probationary year', *British Journal of Educational Psychology*, XXXIV, pp. 75-84.

CORNWELL, J. (1965) *The Probationary Year*, Report published privately by the University of Birmingham Institute of Education.

DALRYMPLE, A. H. (1967) 'The In-Service Training of Probationary Teachers', *Education for Teaching*, No. 73, pp. 48-52.

EDMONDS, E. L. (1961) 'Problems of School Inspection', *Researches and Studies*, XXII, pp. 28-43.

EDMONDS, E. L. (1967) *The First Year of Teaching*, London: N.U.T.

ELDRIDGE, G. and Young Teachers (1964) 'Gossamers & Cobwebs', *The New Era*, Nos. 1, 2 and 3.

FLOUD, J. (1962) 'The Teacher in an Affluent Society', *British Journal of Sociology*, XIII, pp. 229-309.

HARGREAVES, D. H. (1967) *Social Relations in a Secondary School*, London: Routledge & Kegan Paul.

HOVLAND, C. I. et al. (1966) 'A Summary of Experimental Studies in Opinion Change', *Attitudes*, Ed. JAHODA, M. and WARREN, N., London: Penguin Books.

KITSON, G. (1966) 'The Leicester Conference', *Forum*, VIII, 2, pp. 46-48.

KLEIN, J. (1961) *Working with Groups*, London: Hutchinson.

KOSKENNIEMI, M. (1965) *Development of Young Elementary School Teachers*, Helsinki: University of Helsinki.

MEADE, J. P. and GREIG, F. W. (1966) *Supervisory Training. A New Approach for Management*, London: H.M.S.O.

MOELLER, G. H. and CHARTERS, W. W. (1965) 'Relation of Bureaucratization to Sense of Power Among Teachers', *Administrative Science Quarterly*, X, pp. 444-465.

MORRIS, J. M. (1966) *Standards and Progress in Reading: studies of children's reading standards and progress in relation to their individual attributes, home circum-*
96

stances and primary school conditions, London: National Foundation for Educational Research.

NICHOLSON, C. (1965) 'A Kind of Guidance', *The New Era*, Nos. 3, 4 and 5.

N.U.S. and N.U.T. (1967) *Teachers on Probation*, London.

N.U.T. and A.T.C.D.E. (1961) *Teachers in their first posts*, London.

PEARCE, W. M. (1959) 'A Follow-up Study of Training College Students', *Education for Teaching*, No. 48, pp. 41-48.

PHILLIPS, M. (1965) *Small Social Groups in England*, London: Methuen.

REVANS, R. W. (1964) *Standards for Morale, Cause and Effect in Hospitals*, London: Nuffield Provincial Hospitals Trust.

RICHARDSON, E. (1967) *Group Study for Teachers*, London: Routledge & Kegan Paul.

RUDD, W. G. A. and WISEMAN, S. (1962) 'Sources of Dissatisfaction Among a Group of Teachers', *The British Journal of Educational Psychology*, XXXII, pp. 275-291.

SEALEY, L. G. W. (1966) 'The Local Authority and the Probationer', *Forum*, VIII, 2, pp. 55-57.

SOFER, C. (1961) *The Organisation from Within: a comparative study of a social institution based on a socio-therapeutic approach*, London: Tavistock.

TAYLOR, P. H. (1962) 'Children's Evaluation of Characteristics of the Good Teacher', *British Journal of Educational Psychology*, XXXII, pp. 258-266.

TUDHOPE, W. B. (1942) 'A Study of the Training College Final Teaching Mark as a Criterion of Future Success in the Teaching Profession', *British Journal of Educational Psychology*, XII, pp. 167-171.

WALLER, W. (1932) *The Sociology of Teaching*, New York: Wiley. (Reprinted in paperback, 1965, New York Science Edition.)

WILSON, B. R. (1962) 'The Teacher's Rôle. A Sociological

Anaysis', *British Journal of Sociology*, XIII, pp. 15-32.

WISEMAN, S. and START, K. B. (1965) 'A Follow-up on Teachers Five Years after completing their training', *British Journal of Educational Psychology*, XXXV, pp. 342-367.

WRIGHT, D. S. (1962) 'A Comparative Study of the Adolescent's Concept of his Parents and Teachers', *Educational Review*, XIV, pp. 226-232.

YOUNG, P. (1967) *The Student and Supervision in Social Work Education*, London: Routledge & Kegan Paul.